25 GRAPHICS PROGRAMS
IN MICROSOFT® BASIC

25 GRAPHICS PROGRAMS IN MICROSOFT® BASIC

BY TIMOTHY J. O'MALLEY

TAB BOOKS Inc.
BLUE RIDGE SUMMIT, PA 17214

NOTICE: MICROSOFT is a registered trademark of Microsoft Corporation.

FIRST PRINTING

Copyright © 1983 by TAB BOOKS Inc.
Printed in the United States of America

Library of Congress Cataloging in Publication Data

O'Malley, Timothy J.
25 graphics programs in microsoft BASIC.

Includes index.
1. Computer graphics.   2. Basic (Computer program
language)   I. Title.   II. Title: Twenty-five graphics
programs in microsoft BASIC.
T385.043   1983   001.55'3   82-19368
ISBN 0-8306-0133-3
ISNB 0-8306-0533-9 (pbk.)

Contents

Preface

Graphics are one of the most interesting applications of microcomputers. Video games are one very obvious example. Graphics do more than just enable us to play games. Graphics allow us to design and test models without actually building anything. The versatility of the computer allows us to create simulations that reflect the performance of the actual model.

But what are graphics and what is the scope of this book? Graphics, in its broadest sense, is the representation of data in a visual form rather than in a numerical or written form. Graphics include everything from graphs to pictures to abstract art. You name it; if it's visual, it's graphic. Specifically this book covers graphics that are written in Microsoft BASIC primarily for use on microcomputers. The programs in this book do not purport to cover all areas of graphics but they give a cross section of some of the applications available to the microcomputer user and programmer. They include bar graphs, two-dimensional graphs, art, three-dimensional graphics, and others. All of the programs that appear in the book were actually run on a microcomputer, and all the figures were printed by a dot matrix printer.

Who can use this book? This book and its programs are self-explanatory. For example, we discuss several techniques for making three-dimensional figures before the relevant programs are presented. This book could be used in a classroom situation or as supplementary reading because it is designed to be an educational tool. It can be used by the designer who wishes to see what a product will look like without actually building it. Some of the programs might be used or be of interest to architects. Whoever uses the programs should have a working knowledge of BASIC.

The programs, which are written in Microsoft BASIC, may be used with slight changes on any given microcomputer that uses a Microsoft BASIC interpreter for its operating system. They are the best programs in BASIC for their specific application; they do not use functions that are peculiar to a particular manufacturer's version of BASIC. In short, they are written in the BASIC used by most microcomputers today.

It is my hope and intention that these programs will help you as a programmer and user to utilize your computer and your talents to their fullest. I would like to thank TAB BOOKS for their generous help and support in getting this book print.

This book is dedicated to anyone who will take a simple idea to its furthest limit: may you find the significance of doing it.

Chapter 1

Introduction to Graphics

Personal computers are capable of many functions: they can control home appliances, synthesize music, listen, talk, calculate biorhythms, compute complicated algorithms, and they can display graphics. Graphics are one of the most fascinating applications of computers because the output is in a form that is easily recognizable by everyone; it's visual. Since human beings are sight-oriented creatures, it makes perfect sense to display computer output in a visual form.

GRAPHICS: THE VISUAL MEDIUM

An old adage says, "a picture is worth a thousand words." This comment is still true today. Computers can be used to draw not only pictures but all kinds of graphs and plots as well as animated figures. This ability makes them invaluable as a graphic tool.

Generally speaking, anything visual can be included in the category of graphics. We can think of graphics as an intelligent arrangement of points. These points can simply be black and white dots or a spectrum of colored dots. Collectively they comprise a graphic image. Because computers can reproduce and generate a series of points, they lend themselves readily to graphics. Since computers can manipulate these points, they are also useful for animated graphics.

Advantages of Pictures

Why are pictures so useful? Because everyone, even the smallest child, knows what a picture represents. A picture is a realistic representation of a collection of objects. We quite naturally relate to pictures.

Pictures can be simple diagrams or figures or they can be complex images. They can be realistic or they can be abstract. They can also be imaginary. Whatever their nature, they convey an almost instantaneous meaning.

Using Computers for Graphics

What kinds of images can computers create?

1

The answer lies with the sophistication of the computer system and the imagination of the programmer. Practically speaking, the images run the gamut from simple black-and-white still figures to animated scenes in full color. As one increases in graphic sophistication, larger computers are required.

Personal computers of modest size are capable of some rather interesting graphics. Almost every computer can draw a graph of some kind. Most are able to display the graphics necessary for a visual game, given the proper programming. Computers with sound and color can augment the realism of the visual display. An imaginary world in microcosm can be created within the memory of the personal computer. Again, the kinds of applications depend on the capability of the computer system and the imagination and talent of the programmer.

MATHEMATICAL DEFINITIONS USED IN GRAPHICS

All computers process numerical data. The job of the programmer is to write an algorithm in a language that the computer can interpret and to use that algorithm to transform numerical data into visual data. Consequently, a fundamental understanding of mathematics is required.

Points, Lines, Curves, Planes

All images are made of points. Sometimes it's more convenient to think in terms of the individual points themselves, as in an X-Y plot. For computers, a point is the smallest dot that the computer can display on the video display screen. The position of that point relative to other points would give that point its meaning. On some systems a point would be a tiny rectangle illuminated on the screen. On other systems a point would be a graphic character with a dot lit (on a visual screen) or printed (on paper). Still others might simply use a period, plus sign, or lowercase "o" to designate a point on a graph (see Fig. 1-1).

Lines are simply a linear arrangement of points. Lines can be vertical or horizontal, or at any angle in between. They are drawn by placing appropriate graphic characters at specific print positions on a screen or paper (see Fig. 1-1). The computer program would control what character to print and where it should be placed.

Curves are lines with variable linearity. Curves, like lines, are computed and plotted by software. To draw a circle, for instance, the computer would plot all points a given distance from a specific coordinate.

Planes are all points within a specified boundary. The boundary might be intersecting lines or curves. A plane might be drawn as all the points within a given distance from a specific coordinate on the surface.

Graphs and Plots

Graphs and plots are very similar. We can think of plots as figures containing a set of points, as on an X-Y plot. Graphs could include figures like the bar graph (histogram), where rectangles are positioned along an axis. The difference is trivial.

Plots can have more than two axis, i.e., more than two dimensions. The third dimension might be at a given angle relative to the other axes. This would give a three-dimensional effect which might make the image more realistic.

Pictures

Mathematical pictures can be made by positioning figures defined mathematically on the video display. A simple example might be a game board, such as a chessboard or a backgammon board. As the game is played, pieces are moved on or removed from the board. Animated graphic figures are another case, however. Generally the more advanced the graphics, the more heavily you must rely on the computer for generating the pictures.

TYPES OF COMPUTER GRAPHICS

Let's now turn our attention to some types of graphics. There are artistic works created by programmers as a form of self-expression. There are realistic graphics, which attempt to depict the world as we see it and there are abstract graphics, which are exaggerations of reality. There are noninteractive graphics, which we cannot adjust or change, and there are interactive graphics, which we can change.

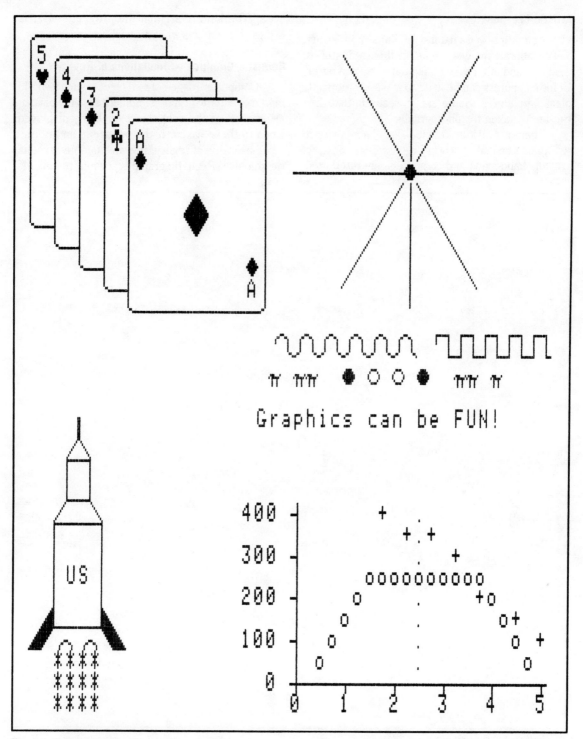

Fig. 1-1. Some examples of computer graphics.

Artistic Creations

Computers are a natural medium for video art. Very elaborate images can be synthesized, stored, modified and otherwise manipulated by computer. Color computers can be used to make aesthetically pleasing pictures. Some are so realistic that they can be mistaken for photographs.

There are all kinds of video art. There are still works and animated works, realistic and abstract art, and hand-made and computer-generated crea-tions. The kind of art that the programmer-artist makes depends on what he wishes to convey.

Realistic Graphics—Simulations of Reality

Computer images of real objects such as build-ings are realistic graphics. Sometimes only particu-lar aspects of the real object might be displayed. Even in these cases, if the picture is an accurate representation of reality, it is an example of realis-tic graphics. Realistic graphics attempt to look like

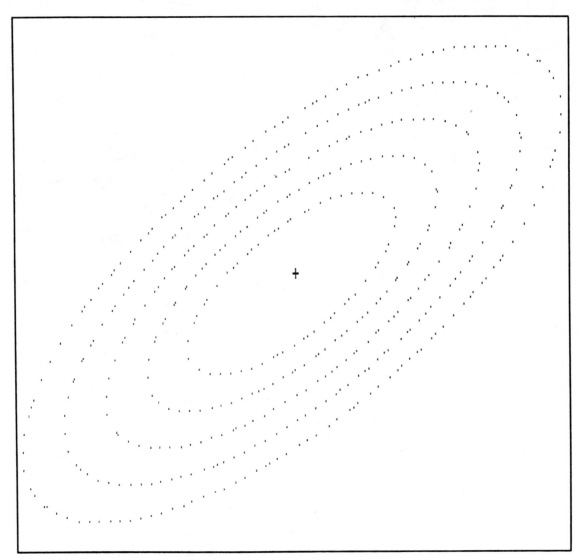

Fig. 1-2. Abstract graphics, orbiting objects.

Fig. 1-3. Abstract graphics, moire patterns.

the objects that they represent. Figure 1-1 also shows realistic playing cards, for example.

Abstract Graphics—Exaggerations of Reality

Abstract graphics are another story. Like abstract art, they are distortions of the real world, altered so as to highlight some feature, perhaps. Figure 1-2 shows five sets of points which form concentric rings about a cross at the center. This image might represent orbiting objects. Figure 1-3, which looks like moire patterns, is even more abstract. Abstract images can be made from realistic images by using programming that modifies some feature of the realistic object.

Noninteractive Graphics

When a programmer is behind a keyboard console, he can sometimes change what he sees instantaneously and sometimes he can not. If he can't readily change the display, he is using noninteractive graphics. Digitized portraits of someone and the figures that we have seen already are examples of noninteractive graphics.

Interactive Graphics—Controlling What You See

Interactive graphics are far more interesting than the noninteractive variety, because you are actively involved with what is happening on the display screen. Any video game player can tell you that. Games are not the only application of interactive graphics. You can use your computer as a sketchpad with the proper programming. By typing certain keys you can draw lines, add color (with color computers), or shade areas. This is called "painting". There are any number of possibilities with interactive computer graphics. The limits are determined only by your imagination and your willingness to pursue an idea to its logical conclusion.

Chapter 2

Two-Dimensional Graphing

One of the easiest ways to represent numbers visually is to construct a graph or plot. On a graph, like a bar graph, a number is equivalent to a length of a line. On a plot a number is a point with a particular position. Since these figures are drawn on a flat surface with axes that are perpendicular, we call them two dimensional graphs.

HISTOGRAMS: PLOTTING
AN ORDERED SET OF NUMBERS

Let's say that a realtor wanted to compare the number of houses that he sold each month over 12 months. First he would obtain the number sold each month, starting with the first month and going through the last month. He would then have an ordered set of numbers. To compare these numbers to themselves, he might construct a bar graph or histogram. Then he would have a visual idea of how each month compared.

The histogram is a graph that has bars running either vertically or horizontally along some axis. Each line represents some number or element in a set of numbers. Usually there is a scale present. The bars might be narrow if there are many numbers or wide if there are few numbers. The bars may be colored to provide contrast. Bar graphs are generally titled to provide explanations. They may or may not start at zero.

Histograms are used to show comparisons. Our realtor, in the example, might notice trends if he made a histogram for each of several years. He might notice that not only do houses sell poorly during the winter months, but when compared to prior years, the number of houses sold decreased. The histogram helps him by making a basis for comparison and providing a visual image of his sales. He might then alter his business practices.

Let's jump right into an example of a BASIC program that makes a histogram. We will look at two similar histogram programs and then at a program that produces a two dimensional plot of points.

Figure 2-1 shows a histogram using the uppercase H as the graphic character. Twelve numbers that have values ranging from three to eight are

	1	2	3	4	5	6	7	8	9	10	11	12
8			HHH									
7.79167			HHH									
7.58333			HHH									
7.375			HHH									
7.16667			HHH									
6.95833			HHH			HHH			HHH			
6.75			HHH			HHH			HHH			
6.54167			HHH			HHH			HHH			
6.33333			HHH			HHH			HHH			
6.125			HHH			HHH			HHH			
5.91667		HHH	HHH			HHH			HHH			HHH
5.70833		HHH	HHH			HHH			HHH			HHH
5.5		HHH	HHH			HHH			HHH			HHH
5.29166		HHH	HHH			HHH			HHH			HHH
5.08333		HHH	HHH			HHH			HHH			HHH
4.875	HHH	HHH	HHH			HHH			HHH		HHH	HHH
4.66666	HHH	HHH	HHH			HHH			HHH		HHH	HHH
4.45833	HHH	HHH	HHH			HHH			HHH		HHH	HHH
4.25	HHH	HHH	HHH			HHH			HHH		HHH	HHH
4.04166	HHH	HHH	HHH			HHH			HHH		HHH	HHH
3.83333	HHH	HHH	HHH	HHH		HHH		HHH	HHH	HHH	HHH	HHH
3.625	HHH	HHH	HHH	HHH		HHH		HHH	HHH	HHH	HHH	HHH
3.41666	HHH	HHH	HHH	HHH		HHH		HHH	HHH	HHH	HHH	HHH
3.20833	HHH	HHH	HHH	HHH		HHH		HHH	HHH	HHH	HHH	HHH
3	HHH	HHH	HHH	HHH	HHH	HHH	HHH	HHH	HHH	HHH	HHH	HHH

READY

Fig. 2-1. Histogram using the uppercase H.

plotted. Each bar is three characters wide and there is a space between the bars. The bars are proportional to the values of each number above the value of three. Alternately, we could have had zero as the lower limit on the Y axis. The listing for this program follows.

```
10 REM              HISTOGRAM GRAPHING PROGRAM
20 REM           WRITTEN BY TIMOTHY J. O'MALLEY
30 REM
40 GOSUB 200:REM    DATA READING SUBROUTINE
50 GOSUB 300:REM    DATA SORTING SUBROUTINE
60 GOSUB 400:REM    HISTOGRAM PRINTING SUBROUTINE
70 END
100 REM             DATA FOR HISTOGRAM
110 DATA 12:REM    THIS IS N, THE NUMBER OF ELEMENTS IN SET
120 DATA 5, 6, 8, 4, 3, 7, 3, 4, 7, 4, 5, 6
130 REM            LINE 120 IS THE ORDERED SET OF N ELEMENTS
```

```
200 REM              DATA READING SUBROUTINE
210 READ N:REM       THIS IS THE NUMBER OF ELEMENTS IN SET
220 DIM X(N):REM     ALLOCATE SPACE IN MEMORY FOR SET X
230 FOR J=1 TO N:REM LINES 230-250 READ DATA INTO SET
240 READ X(J)
250 NEXT J
260 RETURN
300 REM              DATA SORTING SUBROUTINE
310 MIN=X(1):REM     ASSIGN ARBITRARY MINIMUM VALUE OF SET
320 MAX=X(1):REM     ASSIGN ARBITRARY MAXIMIM VALUE OF SET
330 FOR J=1 TO N:REM LINES 330-360 FIND REAL MIN AND MAX
340 IF X(J)<MIN THEN MIN=X(J)
350 IF X(J)>MAX THEN MAX=X(J)
360 NEXT J
370 RETURN
400 REM              HISTOGRAM PRINTING SUBROUTINE
410 WID=64:REM       MAXIMUM WIDTH OF HISTOGRAM
420 HGT=30:REM       MAXIMUM HEIGHT OF HISTOGRAM
430 C$="H":REM       GRAPHIC CHARACTER TO BE USED
440 PRINT CHR$(12);:REM CLEARS VIDEO SCREEN
450 S=8:REM          ALLOW SPACE FOR ORDINATE SCALE
460 IF N>(WID-S) THEN PRINT "TOO MANY NUMBERS":RETURN
470 L=INT((WID-S)/(N+1)):REM ASSIGN WIDTH TO BARS IN GRAPH
480 SP=INT(LOG(MAX-MIN))*(MAX-MIN)/N:REM ORDINATE INCREMENT
490 IF (MAX-MIN)/SP*2<(HGT-4) THEN SP=SP/2:GOTO 490
500 FOR K=MAX TO MIN-SP STEP -SP
510 FOR J=1 TO N
520 IF J=1 THEN PRINT K;:REM PRINT ORDINATE VALUE
530 PRINT TAB(J*L+S);:REM TAB TO EACH BAR IN GRAPH
540 IF X(J)>=K THEN FOR M=1 TO L-1:PRINT C$;:NEXT M
550 NEXT J
560 PRINT
570 NEXT K
580 PRINT
590 IF L<=2 THEN RETURN:REM TOO MANY ELEMENTS TO PRINT SCALE
600 FOR J=1 TO N:REM LINES 600-620 PRINT ABSCISSA SCALE
610 PRINT TAB(J*L+S+SGN((L-3)/2)*(L-3)/2);J;
620 NEXT J
630 RETURN
READY
```

Let's look at the program line by line. Lines 10-30 are remark statements stating the nature and author of the program. Remarks are useful to help identify programs and explain lines. Use them when writing your own programs. Line 40 goes to a subroutine that reads data. Line 50 directs the computer to a subroutine that sorts the data and finds the maximum and minimum values of the data entered. This is used to compute an appropriate scale. Line 60 prints out the histogram using the subroutine that starts at line 400. Line 70 ends the program.

Line 100 is a remark statement used as a header for lines 100-130. Line 110 has a data statement and then a remark statement explaining it. It says that there are 12 elements in the ordered set that the computer will read to make the histogram. Line 120 is the data statement with the 12 values that we will use. Line 130 is a remark statement describing line 120.

Line 200 is a remark statement heading the subroutine that actually reads the data contained in lines 100-130. Line 210 is a read statement and a remark statement. It reads the first value that it finds in the first data statement that it can find in the program. That data statement is in line 110. It assigns that value to the variable named N. Notice that a colon separates two statements that are on the same line and that the remark statement is last. Reason? The computer ignores anything after a remark on a line. Line 220 is a dimension statement that allocates space in memory for the twelve values that we want to graph. Specifically it creates a vector (a linear array) called X consisting of N elements. The remark statement on the same line explains this. Lines 230-250 contain a "loop" that reads the twelve values from available and unused data statements. It creates a variable called J to be used as a counter. J is originally set at 1 and will count up to N, which is 12. Line 240 is a read statement that places a 5 (from line 120) into the set X at the J (initially the first) position. Line 250 is a next statement and seeks to increment the variable J. If J has increased to the value N, it will direct the computer to go on to the next line, line 260. At this point J has the value, 1, so the computer will direct control to the first line number after the for statement, line 240, to read more data. J will have been increased to 2 before line 240 is executed, however. Line 240 then enters the value 6 into the second position of set X. This process continues until J is equal to N, when the return statement in line 260 directs control back to line 50, the subroutine being completed.

Line 50 calls the subroutine starting at line 300, which sorts the data entered in set X. Lines 300 is a remark statement describing lines 300-370. Line 310 assigns the first value in set X to a variable called MIN. We will use this value as a basis of comparison when finding the lowest number in the set. Line 320 assigns the first value in set X to a variable called MAX. MAX is a value that will hold the largest number of set X. Lines 330-360 are another loop. We will use the same variable, J, for a counter. This loop finds the true maximum and minimum values in set X. Line 340 contains an if statement that says if the Jth element in set X is less than the value of MIN, assign that value to MIN. MIN is now equal to the value of X(J). Line 350 says if the Jth value of set X is greater than the value of MAX, increase the value of MAX to be equal to the Jth value of X. Line 360 is a next statement which will increase the counter, J, up to the value N and send control back to the first statement after the for statement, line 340. If J is already equal to N, control goes to line 370, which is a return statement. This statement directs control back to line 60 because the subroutine is completed.

Line 60 calls the subroutine that starts at line 400. This subroutine actually prints out the histogram. Line 400 is a remark that describes the subroutine. Line 410 assigns the value of 64 to a variable called WID. The remark statement on that line explains that this value will be used when scaling the maximum width of the histogram. If your video screen is less than 64 characters wide, you might want to change WID to a smaller value, say 32 or 40. Line 420 assigns the value of 30 to the variable HGT, which is used to scale the height of the bar graph. Line 430 assigns the literal character, H, to the string variable, C$. This string variable contains the literal character to be used to draw the bars in the graph, as the remark on that line says. Line 440 causes the computer to print the character that has an ASCII code of 12. 12 is the code for the form feed on printers. It will also clear the video screen completely. Some computers can use the command CLS for the same purpose. PRINT CHR$(12); will work on more computers, though. The semicolon in this statement keeps the print position on the same line after the clear. That position is in the upper left corner of the video screen.

Line 450 assigns the value 8 to the variable named S. S is the number of spaces that we will allow the computer to print for the numbers of the ordinate (Y) axis. Line 460 is an if statement that says if N is greater than the width minus S, an error message stating that there are too many numbers to make bars for will be printed, and control will return to line 70, which is the end statement. Line 470 assigns the value of $INT((WID-S)/(N+1))$ to the variable L. INT is the integer command and rounds fractional numbers down to next integer. L is the width, in characters, that each bar will be in the graph. Line 480 attempts to divide the vertical axis into as many reasonably spaced increments as possible still using as much height as it can. SP could alternately be assigned a specific value if you'd like. Line 490 says that if the value assigned to SP in line 480 is too large (making too many lines), divide the value of SP in half and then go to line number 490 again to see if SP is still too large. If it is, it will be divided in half and checked again. Eventually SP will be made small enough to work and the computer will go on to line 500.

Line 500 is the start of a loop with a counter, K, assigned initially to the value equal to MAX. The value of K in this case will decrease to the value MIN−SP by steps (or increments) of −SP. Line 510 is another loop inside the K loop, and uses the variable J as a counter. These loops are said to be "nested." J will go from 1 to N. The J loop will be executed many times because it is inside the K loop. The K loop is for the rows and the J loop is for the columns. Line 520 says that if J is equal to 1, print the value of K and stop the print head in that position (because of the semicolon). Line 530 is a print tab statement that moves the print position to the J*L+S position and stops it there. Line 540 says if X(J) is greater than or equal to K, print L−1 graphic characters and stop the print head. This is accomplished by yet another nested loop, the M loop. Not all versions of BASIC allow for the if-then—for-next combination so be careful. Line 550 terminates the J loop if J gets larger than N. Line 560 causes the print head to be moved to the beginning of the next line. (Remember the semicolons holding the print head at specific positions?) Line 570 either increases K or terminates the K loop. Line 580 is a simple print statement that puts a space between the bars and the X axis scaling numbers. Line 590 says that if L is less than or equal to two, skip the printing of the abscissa scale because there are too many elements in the set to print an index for each of them. Control will return to line 70 which will end the program.

Lines 600-620 print the abscissa scale underneath the bars in the graph. The J loop goes from 1 to N. Line 610 will tab to the approximate center of the bar, print the index (the value of J), and hold the print head in that position. Line 620 will then increment J and go back to line 610 to print the next number under the next bar. This loop continues until J exceeds the value N. Line 630 will return control to line 70, which ends the program. That's it! The modified program listing follows.

```
10 REM              HISTOGRAM GRAPHING PROGRAM
20 REM          WRITTEN BY TIMOTHY J. O'MALLEY
30 REM
40 GOSUB 200:REM    DATA READING SUBROUTINE
50 GOSUB 300:REM    DATA SORTING SUBROUTINE
60 GOSUB 400:REM    HISTOGRAM PRINTING SUBROUTINE
80 GOSUB 1000:REM   OPTIONAL SCREEN DUMP TO PRINTER
90 END
100 REM             DATA FOR HISTOGRAM
110 DATA 12:REM     THIS IS N, THE NUMBER OF ELEMENTS IN SET
120 DATA 5, 6, 8, 4, 3, 7, 3, 4, 7, 4, 5, 6
130 REM             LINE 120 IS THE ORDERED SET OF N ELEMENTS
200 REM             DATA READING SUBROUTINE
```

```
210 READ N:REM        THIS IS THE NUMBER OF ELEMENTS IN SET
220 DIM X(N):REM      ALLOCATE SPACE IN MEMORY FOR SET X
230 FOR J=1 TO N:REM LINES 230-250 READ DATA INTO SET
240 READ X(J)
250 NEXT J
260 RETURN
300 REM               DATA SORTING SUBROUTINE
310 MIN=X(1):REM      ASSIGN ARBITRARY MINIMUM VALUE OF SET
320 MAX=X(1):REM      ASSIGN ARBITRARY MAXIMIM VALUE OF SET
330 FOR J=1 TO N:REM LINES 330-360 FIND REAL MIN AND MAX
340 IF X(J)<MIN THEN MIN=X(J)
350 IF X(J)>MAX THEN MAX=X(J)
360 NEXT J
370 RETURN
400 REM               HISTOGRAM PRINTING SUBROUTINE
410 WID=60:REM        MAXIMUM WIDTH OF HISTOGRAM
420 HGT=30:REM        MAXIMUM HEIGHT OF HISTOGRAM
430 C$=CHR$(177):REM GRAPHIC CHARACTER TO BE USED
440 PRINT CHR$(12);:REM CLEARS VIDEO SCREEN
450 S=8:REM           ALLOW SPACE FOR ORDINATE SCALE
460 IF N>(WID-S) THEN PRINT "TOO MANY NUMBERS":RETURN
470 L=INT((WID-S)/(N+1)):REM ASSIGN WIDTH TO BARS IN GRAPH
480 SP=INT(LOG(MAX-MIN))*(MAX-MIN)/N:REM ORDINATE INCREMENT
490 IF (MAX-MIN)/SP*2<(HGT-4) THEN SP=SP/2:GOTO 490
500 FOR K=MAX TO MIN-SP STEP -SP
510 FOR J=1 TO N
520 IF J=1 THEN PRINT K;:REM PRINT ORDINATE VALUE
530 PRINT TAB(J*L+S);:REM TAB TO EACH BAR IN GRAPH
540 IF X(J)>=K THEN FOR M=1 TO L-1:PRINT C$;:NEXT M
550 NEXT J
560 PRINT
570 NEXT K
580 PRINT
590 IF L<=2 THEN RETURN:REM TOO MANY ELEMENTS TO PRINT SCALE
600 FOR J=1 TO N:REM LINES 600-620 PRINT ABSCISSA SCALE
610 PRINT TAB(J*L+S+SGN((L-3)/2)*(L-3)/2);J;
620 NEXT J
630 RETURN
1000 REM         OPTIONAL SCREEN DUMP TO PRINTER
1010 DIM VA(30,60):FOR J=1 TO 30:FOR K=1 TO 60
1020 VA(J,K)=PEEK(64*(J-1)+K-3969):NEXT K,J
1030 N1=3*2^INT(6*RND(1)):REM USE RANDOM PIN
1040 POKE 260,0:POKE 261,0:POKE 0,62:POKE 1,27
1050 POKE 2,205:POKE 3,12:POKE 4,224:POKE 5,201
1060 XX=USR(0):POKE 1,65:XX=USR(0):POKE 1,2:XX=USR(0)
1070 FOR J=1 TO 30:FOR L=-8 TO -1
```

```
1080 FOR K=0 TO 59:IF K/15=INT(K/15) THEN GOSUB 1120
1090 CN=PEEK(L-8*(255-VA(J,K+1))):FOR M=7 TO 0 STEP -1
1100 POKE 1,N1*SGN(CN AND 2^M):XX=USR(0):NEXT M,K
1110 POKE 1,13:XX=USR(0):NEXT L,J:POKE 1,12:XX=USR(0):RETURN
1120 POKE 1,27:XX=USR(0):POKE 1,75:XX=USR(0)
1130 POKE 1,120:XX=USR(0):POKE 1,0:XX=USR(0):RETURN
READY
```

Now let's consider the altered program. In the second version of this histogram graphing program, we will change line 430 to assign the literal character whose ASCII code is 177 to the string variable, C$. This is where a lot of computers differ. We want the computer to print a solid rectangle instead of a capital H. A solid rectangle on some computers has an ASCII code of 191 or another number. Check your system's manual. Figure 2-2 shows the histogram printed using a special graphics character. Some computers do not have any special graphic characters at all. In this case you might want to substitute the code for the # sign or the code for the asterisk.

We have also added lines 80 and 90 and deleted line 70. Line 80 calls the subroutine starting at line 1000, which is an optional screen dump. This takes what is located on the screen and prints it on paper. This subroutine is highly system-specific. It depends on the printer that you are using as well. Many manufacturers provide screen dump routines for their computers, so substitute that routine at line 1000. We will go through subroutine starting at line 1000 very briefly now.

Line 1000 is a remark describing the subroutine. Line 1010 dimensions an array called VA. This two-dimensional array consists of 30 rows and 60 columns, corresponding to HGT and WID, respectively. We could also have written it DIM VA(HGT, WID) in some BASICs. We also start a nested J and K loops. Line 1020 looks at what characters are in what positions on the screen and assigns the ASCII codes of those characters to the corresponding positions in the array, VA. The upper left corner on one system has a memory address of −3968, while on another system it has the address of 15360. Systems are not compatible in their memories. Line 1030 assigns one of the

pins on a dot matrix printer to be used in the printing. Again all printers are not alike. Lines 1040-1060 poke a Z-80 machine language subroutine into a reserved section of memory. The rest of this subroutine simply sends the array, VA, to the printer line by line. Don't be overly concerned about understanding it.

Advantages and Disadvantages

Histograms have the advantage of displaying data visually and providing a basis for comparison between elements in a set. Histograms have the disadvantage of being misleading, particularly if the scale does not start at zero. Figure 2-1 starts at 3 and goes to 8. Since it does not start at zero, it might appear at first glance that some of the values are several times those of some of the others; they are not. Sometimes histograms can show an unfair comparison. Trends or the lack of them, may not be reflected in the histogram.

CARTESIAN COORDINATES: PLOTTING TWO DATA SETS

When you have pairs of numbers in a set, it might be useful to plot the numbers as points. Since the numbers may not be evenly distributed on either axis, a histogram would be out of the question. In this case, we need a Cartesian coordinate, or X-Y, plot.

The X-Y plot is a true two-dimensional plot; it has an axis that is at right angles to the other axis. Generally, the horizontal axis is the abscissa, or X axis, and the vertical axis is the ordinate, or Y axis. Points are plotted according to the scale on each axis.

The X-Y plot is very useful for statistical purposes. You can see how points are clustered together, how Y-values change in relationship to

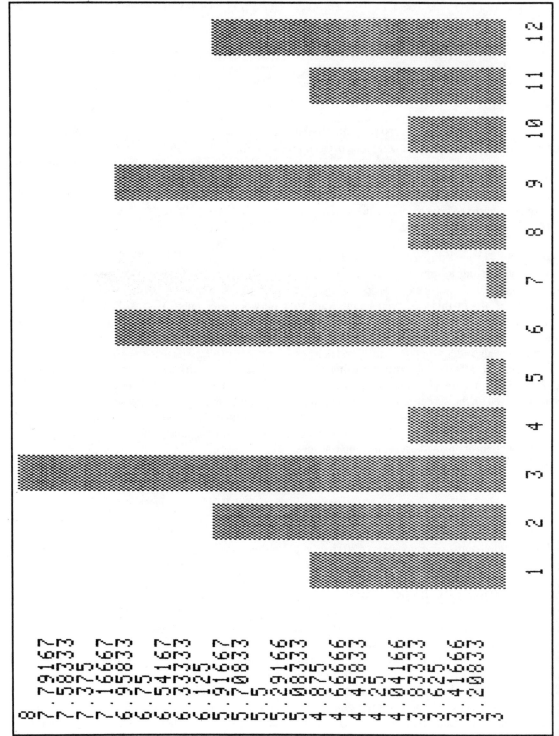

Fig. 2-2. Histogram using graphic characters.

changes in X-values, and how linear the points are. If you can manipulate the independent variable (the abscissa values) and the dependent variable (the ordinate values) is altered as a consequence, you can prove a functional relationship. Plots thus make statistics meaningful.

An Example in BASIC

Let's now look at another BASIC program, one that will plot a two-dimensional figure. Figure 2-3 shows the display of the program. This program plots the percent saturation of hemoglobin as a function of the partial pressure of oxygen in *torr* (units of pressure equal to 1/760 of an atmosphere). Lowercase letter os represent the points plotted. Notice that the computer made titles for the axes and the plot. This plot shows that as the partial pressure of oxygen increases, the percent saturation of hemoglobin increases and asymptomatically approaches 100%.

```
10 REM                    TWO DIMENSIONAL PLOTTER
20 REM                 WRITTEN BY TIMOTHY J. O'MALLEY
30 REM                 COPYRIGHT 1982, TAB BOOKS INC.
40 REM
50 CLEAR 200:REM      INCREASE STRING SPACE FOR TITLES
60 GOSUB 200:REM      DATA READING SUBROUTINE
70 GOSUB 400:REM      DATA SORTING SUBROUTINE
80 GOSUB 600:REM      SCALING AND PLOTTING SUBROUTINE
85 GOSUB 1000:REM (OPTIONAL) SCREEN DUMP TO PRINTER
90 END
100 REM                    DATA FOR PLOTTER
110 DATA OXYGEN DISSOCIATION CURVE:REM THIS IS MAIN TITLE
120 DATA O2 PART. PRES. (TORR):REM THIS IS ABSCISSA TITLE
130 DATA % SAT. OF HB BY O2:REM THIS IS ORDINATE TITLE
140 DATA 10:REM       NUMBER OF (X,Y) PAIRS
150 DATA 10,9.8, 20,32.4, 30,56.4, 40,74.2, 50,83.5
160 DATA 60,89.1, 70,92.6, 80,94.6, 90,96.3, 100,97.3
170 REM                    LINES 150-160 ARE: X1,Y1, X2,Y2, ETC.
180 DATA 0,100,10:REM X-SCALING AS MIN X, MAX X, DIVISIONS
190 DATA 0,100,10:REM Y-SCALING AS MIN Y, MAX Y, DIVISIONS
200 REM                    DATA READING SUBROUTINE
210 READ M$:REM       READ MAIN TITLE
220 READ A$:REM       READ ABSCISSA TITLE
230 READ O$:REM       READ ORDINATE TITLE
240 READ N:REM        READ NUMBER OF (X,Y) PAIRS
250 DIM X(N),Y(N):REM ALLOCATE SPACE IN MEMORY FOR DATA
260 FOR J=1 TO N:REM LINES 260-280 READ DATA PAIRS
270 READ X(J),Y(J)
280 NEXT J
290 READ MNX,MXX,XD:REM READ X-SCALING VARIABLES
300 READ MNY,MXY,YD:REM READ Y-SCALING VARIABLES
310 RETURN
400 REM                 DATA SORTING SUBROUTINE
410 FOR J=1 TO N-1:REM LINES 410-530 SORT BY DECREASING
420 K=J:REM            Y-VALUES THEN BY INCREASING X-VALUES
```

```
430 IF Y(K)>Y(K+1) THEN 530
440 IF Y(K)=Y(K+1) THEN 500
450 A=X(K):X(K)=X(K+1):X(K+1)=A
460 B=Y(K):Y(K)=Y(K+1):Y(K+1)=B
470 K=K-1
480 IF K>=1 THEN 430
490 GOTO 530
500 IF X(K)<=X(K+1) THEN 530
510 A=X(K):X(K)=X(K+1):X(K+1)=A
520 GOTO 470
530 NEXT J
540 MIN=X(1):MAX=X(1):REM LINES 540-580 FIND MINIMUM
550 FOR J=1 TO N:REM        AND MAXIMUM X-VALUES
560 IF X(J)<MIN THEN MIN=X(J)
570 IF X(J)>MAX THEN MAX=X(J)
580 NEXT J
590 RETURN
600 REM                 SCALING AND PLOTTING SUBROUTINE
610 WID=60:REM        MAXIMUM VIDEO SCREEN WIDTH
620 HGT=30:REM        MAXIMUM VIDEO SCREEN HEIGHT
630 C$="o":REM        GRAPHIC CHARACTER USED FOR POINTS
640 PRINT CHR$(12);:REM CLEAR SCREEN (SOME USE CLS)
650 DY=MXY-MNY:REM    RANGE OF Y-VALUES
660 YC=DY/YD:REM      ACTUAL PLOT HEIGHT
670 DX=MXX-MNX:REM    RANGE OF X-VALUES
680 XC=DX/XD:REM      ACTUAL PLOT WIDTH
690 S=5+LEN(STR$(MXY)):REM ORDINATE TITLE AND SCALE SPACE
700 IF (YC*2)<(HGT-6) THEN YC=YC*2:GOTO 700
710 IF (XC*2)<(WID-S) THEN XC=XC*2:GOTO 710
720 PRINT TAB(S+(XC-LEN(M$))/2);M$
730 L=INT((LEN(O$)-YC)/2):P=1:W=S
740 FOR J=MXY TO MNY STEP -DY/YC
750 IF L>0 THEN PRINT MID$(O$,L,1);
760 IF (J/YD)=INT(J/YD) THEN PRINT TAB(2);J;TAB(S-1);"-";
770 PRINT TAB(S);
780 IF P>N THEN 860
790 IF ABS(J-Y(P))>ABS(DY/YC) THEN 860
800 U=S+(X(P)-MNX)/DX*XC
810 IF U<W THEN FOR R=0 TO W-U:PRINT CHR$(1);:NEXT R
820 IF U>W THEN FOR R=1 TO U-W:PRINT CHR$(19);:NEXT R
830 PRINT C$;:REM CHR$(1) IS MOVE PRINT POSITION TO LEFT
840 W=U:P=P+1:REM CHR$(19) IS MOVE PRINT POSITION TO RIGHT
850 IF P<=N THEN 790
860 PRINT
870 L=L+1:W=S
880 NEXT J
```

```
890 FOR K=1 TO 2
900 FOR J=MNX TO MXX STEP XD
910 U=S+(J-MNX)/DX*XC
920 IF K=1 THEN PRINT TAB(U);"'";
930 IF K=2 THEN PRINT TAB(U-INT(LEN(STR$(J)))/2);J;
940 NEXT J
950 PRINT
960 NEXT K
970 PRINT
980 PRINT TAB(S+(XC-LEN(A$))/2);A$
990 RETURN
1000 REM               OPTIONAL SCREEN DUMP TO PRINTER
1010 DIM VA(30,60):FOR J=1 TO 30:FOR K=1 TO 60
1020 VA(J,K)=PEEK(64*(J-1)+K-3969):NEXT K,J
1030 N1=3*2^INT(6*RND(1)):REM USE RANDOM PIN
1040 POKE 260,0:POKE 261,0:POKE 0,62:POKE 1,27
1050 POKE 2,205:POKE 3,12:POKE 4,224:POKE 5,201
1060 XX=USR(0):POKE 1,65:XX=USR(0):POKE 1,2:XX=USR(0)
1070 FOR J=1 TO 30:FOR L=-8 TO -1
1080 FOR K=0 TO 59:IF K/15=INT(K/15) THEN GOSUB 1120
1090 :CN=PEEK(L-8*(255-VA(J,K+1))):FOR M=7 TO 0 STEP -1
1100 POKE 1,N1*SGN(CN AND 2^M):XX=USR(0):NEXT M,K
1110 POKE 1,13:XX=USR(0):NEXT L,J:POKE 1,12:XX=USR(0):RETURN
1120 POKE 1,27:XX=USR(0):POKE 1,75:XX=USR(0)
1130 POKE 1,120:XX=USR(0):POKE 1,0:XX=USR(0):RETURN
READY
```

We now examine the program line by line. Line 10 states the nature of the program with a remark statement. Line 20 states the author and line 30 states that it is copyrighted by TAB Books Inc. Line 40 is a remark statement that is used simply to separate the lines. Line 50 is a clear statement that increases the amount of available string space for string variables to 200 characters. Not all versions of BASIC will do this, so check your particular BASIC. This line also contains a remark statement. Line 60 is a subroutine call to line 200, which reads data for the plot. Line 70 is a call to a subroutine that starts at line 400. That subroutine sorts the data. Line 80 is a subroutine call for scaling and plotting. Line 85 is an optional screen dump for printers. Line 90 ends the program.

Line 100 is a remark statement for lines 100-190, which contains the data for the program. Line 110 contains a data statement and a remark statement, as do lines 120 and 130. Data statements should not contain commas since commas are used to separate data. Line 140 is a data statement informing the computer that the number of (X,Y) pairs will eventually be set to 10 (from line 240). Lines 150 and 160 are the data statements that contain those ten (X,Y) pairs. Line 170 is a remark statement stating that fact. Line 180 states that we want the abscissa scale to go from 0 to 100 by increments of 10. Line 190 says that we want the Y scale to go from 0 to 100 by increments of 10.

Line 200 is a remark statement for the subroutine in lines 200-310, which reads the data into the variables. Line 210 reads the string variable, M$, from the first data statement. This is used for the main title of the plot. You can, of course, change this by changing line 110. Line 220 reads the abscissa title from the next data statement and assigns that to the string variable, A$. Line 230 does a similar thing for the ordinate title, assigning it to the string variable, O$. Line 240 reads the first number, N, which is the number of (X, Y) pairs, from line 140. Line 250 is a dimension statement for the arrays, X and Y. Line 260-280 are a loop that reads in the elements of those arrays. Lines 290 and 300 read the data from lines 180 and 190, respectively. These values are the scaling variables for the plot. Line 310 is a return statement that directs the computer out of the subroutine to line 70.

Line 400 is a remark statement describing the subroutine in lines 400-590, which sorts the data. Lines 410-530 are a modified shell sorting routine that sorts the (X, Y) pairs by decreasing Y-values. If two Y-values are equal, it sorts them by increasing X-values. Line 410 starts the J loop. Line 420 sets K equal to the current value of J. Line 430 says that if the Kth element of Y is greater than the (K+1)th element of Y, go to line 530, which will attempt to increase the J counter and continue the loop. Line 440 says if Y(K) is equal to Y(K+1), go to line 500, which will check to see if the X values are increasing. If the computer has not met either of the logical conditions of lines 430 or 440, it assumes that Y(K) is less than Y(K+1) and it must swap them and their associated X values. Line 450 swaps the X values and line 460 swaps the Y values. Notice that they are first assigned to a variable, A; otherwise X(K) and Y(K) would be lost: X(K) would have been made equal to X(K+1), and Y(K) would have been made equal to Y(K+1). K is then decreased by 1, and line 480 checks to see if K is greater than or equal to 1. If it is, control branches to line 430 to compare the switched values to the last Y value. Line 490 branches to line 530 if the condition in line 480 is not logically true. Line 500 checks to see if the X values are increasing for equal Y values. If they are, control goes to line 530, the next J part of the loop. If the condition in line 500 is false, the X-values in line 510 are swapped and control is sent back to line 470 by the goto statement in line 520. Lines 540-580 find the minimum and maximum X values using a loop. Line 590 ends the subroutine call and control returns to line 80.

Lines 600-990 scale and plot the data as shown in Fig. 2-3. Line 600 is a remark statement for that subroutine. Line 610 sets the width of the plot to a maximum of 60 and line 620 sets the height of the plot to a maximum of 30 characters. Line 630 assigns the lowercase letter o as the graphic character to the string variable C$. Line 640 clears the screen. Line 650 sets the variable DY as the difference between the maximum Y value and the minimum Y value. This value will be used to calculate the appropriate height of the plot. Line 660 assigns YC as the plot height by dividing DY by YD. This may be changed later. Line 670 sets DX as the difference between the maximum X value and the minimum X value. This value will be used to determine the actual plot width. Line 680 sets the plot width. Line 690 sets up space for the ordinate title and scale. Line 700 will keep increasing the value of YC if YC is too small for the height. Line 710 does a similar multiplication on the variable XC for the actual width of the plot.

Line 720 tabs to the approximate center of the plot and then prints the title of the plot, M$. It centers the main title by subtracting the length of one-half of the characters in the title. Line 730 finds the position to center the ordinate title and sets the line number to the variable L. This line also sets the variables P and W.

Lines 740-880 form a loop that draws the rows of the plot. J is set to the maximum Y value and will decrease to the minimum Y value by decrements of −DY/YC. Line 750 says that if L is greater than zero, the Lth character in the ordinate title should be printed. The semicolon will hold the print head at the next position. Line 760 says that if we are on a line that has a scale number, the number and a hyphen should be printed and the print head should be kept in position. Line 770 will tab to the first possible position for a point to be printed. Line 780 says that if there are no points to be plotted on that line, go to line 860, the next row of the figure. Line 790 checks to see if any points are within the row also. If not, control goes to line 860. Line 800 sets V as the exact position of a point on the plot. Line 810 says that if the point is to the left of the print position, move the print position back (W−V+1) spaces. The cursor control code 1 is used. Some

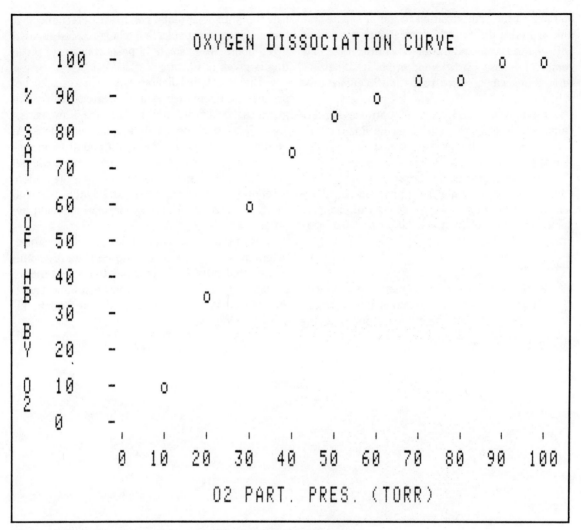

Fig. 2-3. Oxygen dissociation curve, an example of two-dimensional plotting.

computers use **PRINT CHR$(24)** instead to move the cursor back one space without erasing the printed character or number. Check your system. Line 820 says that if the point is to the right of the current position, move the cursor or print head to the right (V-W) spaces by using the control code 19. Again, some computers use the code 25 instead of 19. These actions are accomplished by a nested loop using the variable R. Line 830 prints the graphic character. Line 840 sets the variable W equal to the current print position and P is incremented by one. If P is less than the number of

points to be plotted (in line 850), control goes to line 790 to see if any those points are on the current row of the plot. Line 860 moves to the next row of the plot. Line 870 increases the line number counter and sets the first possible print position variable, W, to the left most part of the plot, S. Line 880 checks for the next row of the plot. It is the next statement of the J loop.

Lines 890-960 form a loop that prints the X axis scale and markings. It computes the proper positions for the apostrophes and attempts to center the numbers under each apostrophe. Line

950 moves the print position to the next line and line 960 ends the K loop. Line 970 puts a space between the scale and the abscissa title. Line 980 centers the abscissa title and prints it. Line 990 returns the computer control to line 85 ending this subroutine.

Lines 1000-1130 form an optional screen dump, which places whatever is on the video screen onto paper. We will not describe it since it is system specific and uses Z-80 machine language.

This completes the description of our two-dimensional plotter. Other programs could be written that would print plots. Later we will examine some examples of high resolution plotting programs.

DIAGRAMS

Personal computers can construct two-dimensional graphs other than histograms and Cartesian coordinate plots. They can construct polar coordinate plots. In polar plots, points are determined by the angle and length of a line that is rotated about a given point. An example of polar coordinate plotting is given in Chapter 6.

Highly detailed diagrams like maps can also be produced on some personal computers with good graphics. Other possibilities include flowcharts, logic circuit diagrams, and floorplans of houses. A personal computer might make a good tool in designing schematic diagrams. Components could be moved, added, and erased while on the video screen. When finished, a print out might be made of the final diagram. Time and paperwork could be saved.

There are probably other two-dimensional diagrams and graphs that could be made by computer. Applications will continue to present themselves as people with varied interests and backgrounds use personal computers. Experiment and see what you find.

Chapter 3

Three-Dimensional Graphing

Three-dimensional graphing is a method of reproducing three-dimensional figures on two-dimensional surface, such as a video screen or on a sheet of paper. There must be a systematic procedure for incorporating the third axis as a function of the other two axes so that the figures acquire a realistic spatial quality.

HOW TO PLOT IN THREE DIMENSIONS

If we assume that the horizontal axis is called X and the vertical axis is called Y, a third axis would be called Z. Often mathematicians consider that the Z values in a graph are a function of the X and Y values. In such case the Z axis would be the vertical axis, the X axis would be the horizontal axis, and the Y axis would be represented in some other way. Let us look at a way to define that other axis.

A simple method would be to have that axis at an angle relative to the other axes. The angle might be 30 or 45 degrees above the horizontal axis. To plot points, you would measure the X value along the horizontal axis, then move along the angle of the Y axis, and then move vertically for the Z axis. The resulting point would be produced as a function of all of these actions. So long as the angle remained constant the points would be accurately placed on the two-dimensional plotting medium. That is a simple solution to three-dimensional graphing.

A more sophisticated solution would involve making the X axis not horizontal, but at a slightly declining angle, and the Y axis at a given angle as before. This produces a plot that is a little more realistic. Again, the points would be placed by travelling along the X axis; then along the Y axis; then vertically along the Z axis the correct number of units.

The first solution just presented is called *oblique projection* while the second is called *axonometric projection*. There are also other methods involving vanishing points to make a perspective graph, but we will not use those methods. Instead, we now briefly look at a perspective method that doesn't use vanishing points.

In this method of doing three-dimensional graphing, the equations, V=F1*ATN(F2*DZ/DY), and $H=F1*ATN(F2*DX/DY)$ are used. V is the vertical position; H is the horizontal position of a point; F1 is a magnification factor; F2 is a perspective factor that distorts the image; DZ is the difference in distance from the viewpoint to the point along the Z axis, DY is the distance along the Y axis; and DX is the difference along the X axis. ATN is the arctangent function in BASIC. When these equations are used for each point plotted, an accurate perspective graph is made without the use of vanishing points. We will investigate these equations further in the next chapter although we will use them in two programs in this chapter.

USING TRANSFORMATION EQUATIONS TO ROTATE IMAGES

When plotting in three dimensions, it is often necessary to rotate the figures so that different views can be presented. It may also be necessary to move the points in some direction. To perform both of these manipulations, you must use transformation equations. We use a set of rotation transformation equations to rotate a set of points around each of the three axes and a set of transformation equations to displace the points along each of three axes. Rotation of points around the Z axis would involve changing the X and Y coordinates of the points, for instance. If we wanted to displace the points along the Z axis, say, five units, we would add five to each of the Z values for all the points involved. The next chapter will go into more detail about rotations in space.

GRAPHING RESOLUTION AND GRAPHIC CHARACTERS

All graphs or plots require some degree of resolution. There are two kinds of graphics that are commonly used today. There are bit image graphics, which use individual dots to make an image, and there are block type graphics. Bit image graphics are composed of rows and columns of dots, some of which are dark. Block graphics are composed of rows and columns of squares, some of which are dark.

Bit image graphics have greater resolution, but many computers designed for personal use today do not have that kind of resolution available for display on a video screen. There are lowcost printers available that will make print high-resolution pictures using bit image graphics.

Some computers use block graphics to place graphics on the screen without using a lot of memory. Certain screen elements, of the block style, would be turned on to comprise the image. Thus graphs, plots, or other images could be produced. Some computers have predefined graphics or user-defined graphics to assist in the production of images.

Computers with graphic capabilities typically use characters that have ASCII codes above 128. When these characters are printed on the video screen, the graphic characters appear. Some computers allow for user-defined graphics so that foreign letters or symbols can be created. This provides a great deal of flexibility in graphing.

Some printers will print user-defined graphics. The state-of-the-art is changing rapidly. Often, however, what a programmer will do is display the graphics on the video screen and have the computer *"dump"* whatever is on the screen onto the paper. As we discussed earlier, the programmer would either buy a software package that would accomplish this or create his own software to do the job.

ELIMINATING HIDDEN LINES AND POINTS

Computers can draw line drawings quite easily, but what requires a great deal of computing is the elimination of lines and points that are not supposed to be seen. This is due to the fact that the computer must be programmed to decide what lines or points are really unseen. Algorithms for accomplishing this do not come easily and those that do generally require a lot of number crunching. Without the elimination of *hidden* lines and points, you would see all the points at once, and the image would be confusing. We will look at a couple of methods to get rid of hidden lines in some programs in this book.

THREE-DIMENSIONAL MODELS OF FUNCTIONS

We now turn our attention to two programs

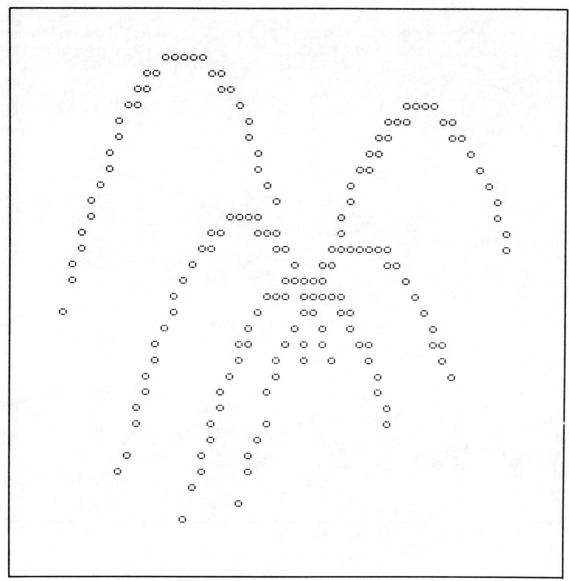

Fig. 3-1. The function Z=X*X− Y*Y, a saddle-shaped figure.

that display three-dimensional functions; one will be in low-resolution and one will be in high resolution. Within the programs we will see one method of eliminating some hidden points.

A Low-Resolution Program In BASIC—Program 4

Figure 3-1 shows the result of plotting the function Z=X*X− Y*Y. A saddle-shaped figure is produced. We showed only some of the points as we will explain later. Notice that it is difficult to see the three-dimensional effect. The image looks more like a spider than anything else. Figure 3-2 has the hidden points of our saddle-shaped function removed. It looks a little more like a three-dimensional figure.

23

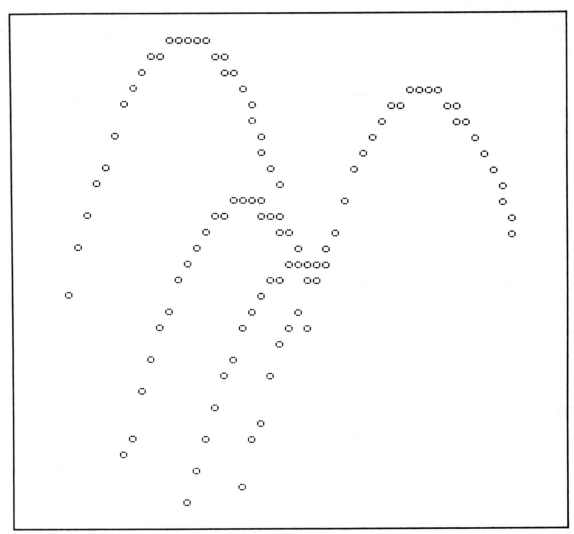

Fig. 3-2. The saddle-shaped function with hidden lines removed.

```
10 REM                  THREE DIMENSIONAL PLOTTER
20 REM                  WRITTEN BY TIMOTHY J. O'MALLEY
30 REM                  COPYRIGHT 1982, TAB BOOKS INC.
40 REM
50 GOSUB 100:REM         DEFINE DATA POINTS
60 GOSUB 300:REM         FIND EXTREME VALUES
70 GOSUB 500:REM         PRINT ON VIDEO SCREEN
80 END
100 REM                 DEFINE DATA POINTS
110 N=500:REM            MAXIMUM NUMBER OF POSSIBLE POINTS
120 DIM V(N),H(N):REM ALLOCATE SPACE FOR COORDINATES
130 C=0:REM              INITIALIZE COUNTER FOR POINTS
```

```
140 FOR X=-2 TO 2:REM DEFINES X-VALUES
150 FOR Y=-2 TO 2 STEP 0.1:REM DEFINES Y-VALUES
160 C=C+1:REM          INCREASE COUNTER
170 Z=X*X-Y*Y:REM    FUNCTION TO BE PLOTTED
180 V(C)=Y*0.5-X*0.26+Z:REM VERTICAL VALUE
190 H(C)=X*0.96+Y*0.87:REM HORIZONTAL VALUE
200 NEXT Y,X
210 RETURN
300 REM                FIND EXTREME VALUES
310 MINV=V(1):MAXV=V(1):REM SET AT ARBITRARY VALUES
320 MINH=H(1):MAXH=H(1):REM SET AT ARBITRARY VALUES
330 FOR J=1 TO C:REM LINES 330-380 FIND MAX AND MIN
340 IF V(J)<MINV THEN MINV=V(J)
350 IF V(J)>MAXV THEN MAXV=V(J)
360 IF H(J)<MINH THEN MINH=H(J)
370 IF H(J)>MAXH THEN MAXH=H(J)
380 NEXT J
390 DV=MAXV-MINV:REM RANGE OF VERTICAL VALUES
400 DH=MAXH-MINH:REM RANGE OF HORIZONTAL VALUES
410 RETURN
500 REM                PRINT ON VIDEO SCREEN
510 WID=64:REM         MAXIMUM SCREEN WIDTH
520 HGT=30:REM         MAXIMUM SCREEN HEIGHT
530 DIM S(HGT,WID):REM DIMENSION SCREEN ARRAY
540 FOR J=1 TO HGT:REM LINES 540-570 FILL ARRAY WITH
550 FOR K=1 TO WID:REM BLANKS, ASCII CODE OF 32
560 S(J,K)=32
570 NEXT K,J
580 FOR J=1 TO C:REM LINES 580-620 FILL ARRAY WITH POINTS
590 HP=INT((H(J)-MINH)/DH*WID+0.5):REM HORIZONTAL POSITION
600 VP=INT((V(J)-MINV)/DV*HGT+0.5):REM VERTICAL POSITION
610 S(VP,HP)=111:REM ASCII CODE FOR LOWERCASE O IS 111
615 GOSUB 800
620 NEXT J
630 PRINT CHR$(12);:REM CLEAR SCREEN (SOME USE CLS)
640 FOR J=HGT TO 1 STEP -1:REM LINES 640-690 PRINT ON SCREEN
650 FOR K=1 TO WID
660 PRINT CHR$(S(J,K));
670 NEXT K
680 PRINT
690 NEXT J
700 RETURN
800 REM                REMOVE POINTS BEHIND PLANE
810 REM    ADD LINE    615 GOSUB 800
820 IF VP<2 THEN RETURN
830 FOR K=VP-1 TO 1 STEP -1
```

```
840 S(K,HP)=32
850 NEXT K
860 RETURN
READY
```

Let's look at the program. Lines 10-40 are remarks that state the nature of the program and the credits. Line 50 is a subroutine call to line 100 for defining the data points. Line 60 is a subroutine call to line 300 to find the extreme points for plotting purposes. Line 70 is a subroutine call to print the figure on the video screen, and line 80 ends the program.

Line 100 is a remark for the first subroutine. Line 110 sets the variable N at 500. This is the maximum number of points that we want to plot. We use this variable in the dimension statements in line 120, which are for the vertical and horizontal positions on the screen. Line 130 sets a counter variable, C, to zero. We then use two nested for-next loops to define the X and Y values used in the function in lines 140 and 150. Line 160 increases the counter. Line 170 computes the value of Z from the current X and Y values. Lines 180 and 190 compute the vertical and horizontal position of point C according to the axonometric projection that we discussed earlier. The Y axis is at 30 degrees above the horizontal, the X axis declines at about 15 degrees below the horizontal, and the Z axis is vertical. The numbers in line 180 are the sines of those degrees and the numbers in line 190 are the cosines of those degrees. Line 200 contains the next statement for the nested loops, and line 210 returns control back to line 60.

Lines 300-410 finds the extreme values for the points. The variables MINH, MAXH, MINV, and MAXV are set at arbitrary first values line lines 310 and 320. Lines 330-380 find the maximum and minimum vertical and horizontal values by using a loop with the variable counter J. Lines 390 and 400 find the range (the difference between the maximum and minimum values of the vertical and horizontal values). Line 410 is a return statement.

Lines 500-700 form the subroutine that prints out the figures. Line 500 is a remark statement.

Line 510 sets the width of the plot to a maximum of 64 characters. You may change this to another value, particularly if your video screen is not 64 characters in width. If your screen is 80 characters wide, you might want to change WID to 80. Line 520 sets the height to 30. You could also change this value to, say, 24. Line 530 is a dimension statement which defines a screen array of height, HGT, and width, WID. We will use this to place points that are to be erased or plotted. Lines 550-570 form a loop that places an ASCII 32 in the entire array. 32 is the ASCII code number for a blank space. We will use this so that the computer will know what to print where there are no points in the array. Lines 580-620 form a loop that fills the S array with points at the proper positions. Lines 590 and 600 adjust the positions in an attempt to use the maximum area of the array. Line 610 sets the array at the location of each point to 111. 111 is the ASCII for the lowercase letter o. If your computer does not have lowercase letters, you might substitute the number, 79, which is the uppercase letter O, or the number 42, which is the code for the asterisk. If you want to erase the hidden points, add line 615, which is a subroutine call to line 800. Line 620 is the next statement of the current loop. Line 630 clears the video screen. The nested loops in lines 640-690 print the characters corresponding to the ASCII codes stored in the S array. Line 700 returns to line 80, which is an end statement.

The subroutine in lines 800-860 erases all points below the current point in the same column of the S array. If the vertical position of the current point is less than 2, line 820 will send control back to the main program, since there could be no points below the current point; we are on the bottom row of the array. Line 830 sets up a loop with the counter K and erases all the possible points below the current position in the same column in the array by setting all the elements to 32, the blank space

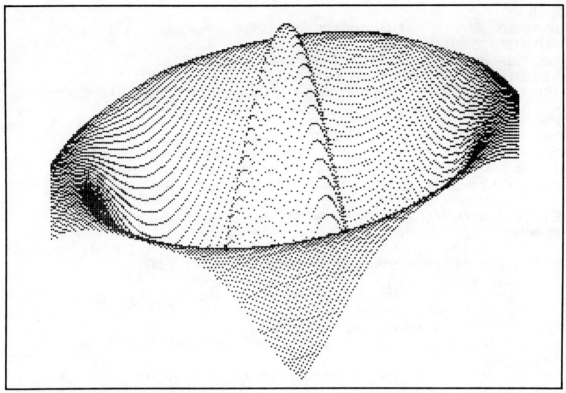

Fig. 3-3. A high-resolution plot of a function.

code. Line 850 terminates the loop, and line 860 is the return statement, which sends control back to line 620.

That's the complete program! To change functions, substitute another line in line 170, which defines the Z-value. Be sure that you have suitable X and Y values or else you might get a domain error (or something to that effect).

A High-Resolution Program in BASIC—Program 5

We now direct our consideration toward another program that plots three-dimensional functions, this one in high-resolution graphics. First of all, to plot in high-resolution, you must either have high-resolution capabilities on your video screen or have a high-resolution printer. Figure 3-3 was printed using a lowcost, high-resolution printer, but it was not displayed on the screen. It was made using a machine-language subroutine that bypassed the BASIC operating system of the microcomputer. We will look at a way to write the entire program using BASIC for ease of comprehension.

```
10 REM          3D HIGH RESOLUTION FUNCTION PLOTTER
20 REM          WRITTEN BY TIMOTHY J. O'MALLEY
30 REM          COPYRIGHT 1982, TAB BOOKS INC.
40 REM
50 GOSUB 100:REM INITIALIZE PROGRAM
60 GOSUB 200:REM PLOT POINTS IN ARRAY
70 GOSUB 600:REM PRINT OUT ARRAY ON PAPER
```

```
80 END
100 REM                INITIALIZE PROGRAM
110 HGT=25:WID=253:W2=127
120 DEF FNA(R)=10*(EXP(-R*R/1000)*COS(R/5))
130 DIM VA(HGT,WID):REM DIMENSION ARRAY FOR PLOT
140 GOSUB 700:REM SET UP MACHINE LANGUAGE SUBROUTINE FOR
    PRINTER
150 RETURN
200 REM              PLOT POINTS IN ARRAY
210 FOR X=-30 TO 30 STEP 0.5:FOR Y=-30 TO 30 STEP 0.2
220 R=SQR(X*X+Y*Y):Z=FNA(R):V=Y*0.17-X*0.08+Z+HGT/2
230 H=X*2.88+Y*2.61+WID/2:IF V<0 OR V>HGT OR H<0 OR
    H>WIDTHEN280
240 IV=INT(V):IH=INT(H):DV=INT(12*(V-IV)):PV=2^DV
250 VA(IV,IH)=VA(IV,IH) OR PV
260 GOSUB 400:REM ERASE POINTS BELOW PV IN VA(IV,IH)
270 GOSUB 500:REM ERASE POINTS BELOW VA(IV,IH)
280 NEXT Y,X:RETURN
400 REM              ERASE POINTS BELOW PV IN VA(IV,IH)
410 IF DV=0 THEN RETURN
420 FOR J=DV-1 TO 0 STEP -1:J2=2^J
430 IF (VA(IV,IH) AND J2)=J2 THEN VA(IV,IH)=VA(IV,IH)-J2
440 NEXT J:RETURN
500 REM              ERASE POINTS BELOW VA(IV,IH)
510 IF IV=0 THEN RETURN
520 FOR J=IV-1 TO 0 STEP -1:VA(J,IH)=0:NEXT J:RETURN
600 REM              PRINT OUT ARRAY ON PAPER
610 FOR JS=HGT TO 0 STEP -1:FOR MS=11 TO 0 STEP -1
620 BS=INT(2^MS):FOR LS=0 TO 1:GOSUB 660
630 FOR KS=LS*W2 TO LS*W2+W2-1:POKE 1,SGN(BS AND VA(JS,KS))
640 XX=USR(0):NEXT KS,LS:POKE 1,13:XX=USR(0):NEXT MS,JS
650 POKE 1,12:XX=USR(0):RETURN
660 POKE 1,27:XX=USR(0):POKE 1,75:XX=USR(0):POKE 1,W2
670 XX=USR(0):POKE 1,0:XX=USR(0):RETURN
700 REM              SET UP MACHINE LANGUAGE SUBROUTINE FOR
    PRINTER
710 POKE 260,0:POKE 261,0:POKE 0,62:POKE 1,27:POKE 2,205
720 POKE 3,12:POKE 4,224:POKE 5,201:XX=USR(0):POKE 1,65
730 XX=USR(0):POKE 1,1:XX=USR(0):RETURN
READY
```

Let's look at the program line by line. Lines 10-40 give the name of the program and other credits using remark statements. Line 50 is a subroutine call to line 100 where the program will be initialized. Line 60 is a subroutine call to line 200, which places points in the array. Line 70 is a call to the subroutine at line 600, which prints out the array on paper. Line 80 ends the program.

Line 100 is a remark, heading the subroutine that sets up (initializes) the program. Line 110 defines the height, HGT, as 25, the width, WID, as 253 and the variable W2 as 127. HGT and WID will be used to dimension the VA array, but there is a very subtle "catch". Each number in that array can represent up to 12 different points. That makes the figure have a height of 12*(25+1) or 312 points maximum, and a width of (253+1) or 254 points maximum. The one extra came from using the 0th index (0,0) of our array for both the rows and columns. All told, they are a maximum of 79,248 positions in which points can be printed. We will see how this is attained later. Line 120 is a defined function that makes the figure. If your computer can not define functions, simply substitute the equivalent of this function when defining Z in line 220. This function contains the exponential function and the cosine function that are predefined in BASIC. Line 130 dimensions the array used in the point plotter. Line 140 is a subroutine call to line 700, which sets up a machine language subroutine to pass numbers to the printer, bypassing the BASIC operating system. Again, we will explain this in detail and show alternate ways to do approximately the same thing in BASIC. Line 150 is a return statement (to line 60).

Line 200 is a remark statement for the plotting subroutine, lines 200-280. Lines 210-280 form nested for-next loops that define the X and the Y values. Line 220 sets the variable R as the square root of X squared plus Y squared. R is the distance from the center of this model. Z is defined as a function of R. R is already a function of X and Y. V, the vertical position of the point, is defined in the same kind of axonometric way that we demonstrated in the last program. In line 230, H is the horizontal position of the point, defined in a similar manner. If H or V are outside the bounds of our array's dimensions, control goes to line 280, which is a next statement for the next set of X and Y coordinates. Line 240 is where it starts to get tricky. In this line we define IV as the integer, or whole number part of the value of V. The same is done for H. Now we define DV as the integer part of 12 times the fractional part of V and we set PV to 2 to the power of DV. That means if the fractional part is zero, PV is 1; if the fractional part is over 0.083, PV is 2; if the fractional part is over 0.167, PV is 4; if the fractional part is 3/12 or more, PV is 8 and so

on up to 11/12 or more where PV equals 2048. Line 250 does a Boolean-algebra binary-logical OR between the array at VA(IV,IH) and PV, and sets the result equal to VA(IV,IH). In this way we can actually represent several points by one number. Make sure your computer can do a binary-logical OR; Type **PRINT 3 OR 1**. Does it equal 3? Line 260 erases all the bits below PV in VA(IV,IH) using its subroutine call to line 400. Line 270 is a subroutine call that erases all numbers below VA(IV,IH) in the same column by going to line 500. Line 280 contains the next stagements for the nested loops and causes a return to line 70 after the loops are completed.

The subroutine in lines 400-440 erases bits in the VA array. Line 400 is a remark statement for the subroutine. Line 410 says if DV is zero, return to the main program because PV is 1 and there are no bits below the bit for the number one. Lines 420-440 use a loop and the Boolean-algebra binary-logical AND operator to find out whether or not if bits exist at certain positions. If your computer works with the OR function in line 250, it will work with the AND function in line 430. Line 420 sets the J counter initially at a value DV-1, to be decreased to zero by decrements of −1. J2 is set to 2 to the power of J. Line 430 says if the bit of the array at VA(IV,IH) exists for the number J2, subtract J2 from the number and redefine VA(IV,IH). This procedure effectively erases a bit if it exists. Line 440 is the next statement for this loop, along with a return statement to line 270.

Lines 500-520 erase all the numbers below VA(IV,IH) in the same column in the VA array. Line 500 is the remark statement for the subroutine. Line 510 says that if we are already at the bottom of the array, forget it and return to line 280. Line 520 contains a loop that says to set all the elements of the array below our current point to zero and then return to line 280.

Lines 600-650 print out the bits of the array on paper. Line 600 is the remark statement for the subroutine and line 610 contains two nested loops, JS, and inside that, MS. JS is for the rows of the array and MS is for the bits of the numbers of the array. Line 620 sets BS equal to the integer of two to the power of MS and contains yet another nested loop inside the MS loop, the LS loop. The LS loop is used to configure the computer to print a line of high-resolution graphics. It does this by going to the subroutine at line 660. Line 630 contains yet another nested for-next loop inside of the LS loop. This loop uses the variable KS for a counter for the columns of the array. Line 630 also contains a poke command. It pokes the sign of the binary logical AND of BS and VA(JS,KS) into memory position 1. Line 640 makes a machine-language subroutine call and prints a possible bit on paper. It then goes to the next KS and LS. Then it pokes the number 13 (code for carriage return) into memory position 1 and does a machine-language subroutine call to send it to the printer. Then the next statement for MS and JS are encountered. Line 650 pokes the number 12 into memory position 1 and sends it to the printer. 12 is the code for the form feed control character. Then the return statement returns control to line 80 to end the program.

Lines 660-670 configure the printer to print the next W2 characters that it receives as high-resolution graphics. These lines are equivalent to: PRINT CHR$(27); CHR$(75); CHR$(W2); CHR$(0). 27 is the code for escape; 75 is the code for "K"; W2 is the number 127 and tells the computer to print the next 127 characters it receives as graphics. The 0 are for characters in excess of 128 (none).

Briefly stated the machine language in lines 700-730 says to LD A with the number at memory location 1, CALL SEND (the memory position to send the contents of A to the current output device)

and return from the machine-language subroutine. Lines 720 and 730 also poke the numbers 65 (for "A"), and 1 to tell the printer that it will be advancing the line by a length equivalent to 1/72". If this makes no sense to you, don't worry about it; this book is about BASIC, not about machine-language.

That concludes the two programs concerning three-dimensional models of functions. We now look at two similar programs that print out space-filling models of molecules, which are presented as spheres.

THREE-DIMENSIONAL, SPACE-FILLING MOLECULAR MODELS

Let's look at two programs that do look realistic; one is a low-resolution program that prints the figure on the video screen and one that creates a high-resolution figure using a printer.

A Low-Resolution Program in BASIC—Program 6

Figure 3-4 shows a series of low-resolution figures depicting two hexagons made of circles. Originally one hexagon ring is tilted "back" into the plane of the page. This model might represent the carbon atoms of the molecule biphenol. We will use this organic molecule to be the model that we will view in the two programs. Figure 3-4 shows the partial rotation of the model about the vertical (Z) axis. Figure 3-5 shows partial rotation about the Y axis; Fig. 3-6 shows partial rotation about the X axis; and Fig. 3-7 shows partial rotation of the left part of the molecule about the X axis.

```
10 REM           LOW-RESOLUTION, SPACE-FILLING
20 REM              ROTATING MOLECULAR MODEL
30 REM           WRITTEN BY TIMOTHY J. O'MALLEY
40 REM           COPYRIGHT 1982, TAB BOOKS INC.
50 REM
60 GOSUB 100:REM INITIALIZE PROGRAM AND READ DATA
70 GOSUB 200:REM SORT BY DECREASING DISTANCES TO VIEWPOINT
80 GOSUB 400:REM PLOT POINTS AND PRINT ON PAPER
90 GOSUB 600:REM ROTATE POINTS ABOUT AN AXIS
95 GOTO 70:REM REPEAT ROTATION AND PRINTING INDEFINITELY
100 REM          INITIALIZE PROGRAM AND READ DATA
110 E=0.4:N1=12:RD=0.5:F=0.1:G=0.98:HGT=64:WID=64
```

```
120 DIM X(N1),Y(N1),Z(N1),U(N1),H(N1),RS(N1),DI(N1),R(3)
130 FOR J=1 TO N1:READ X(J),Y(J),Z(J):NEXT J
140 DATA 0,0,0, 0.5,0,0.87, 1.5,0,0.87, 2,0,0
150 DATA 1.5,0,-0.87, 0.5,0,-0.87, 3,0,0, 3.5,0.348,0.348
160 DATA 4.5,0.348,0.348, 5,0,0, 4.5,-0.348,-0.348
170 DATA 3.5,-0.348,-0.348
190 R(1)=2.5:R(2)=0:R(3)=0:X(0)=2.5:Y(0)=-10:Z(0)=1:B$="Z"
195 RETURN
200 REM          SORT BY DECREASING DISTANCES TO VIEWPOINT
202 FOR J=1 TO N1
204 DY=Y(J)-Y(0):IF DY<=0 THEN PRINT"DECREASE Y(0)":STOP
206 DX=X(J)-X(0):DZ=Z(J)-Z(0)
208 DI(J)=SQR(DY*DY+DX*DX+DZ*DZ):RS(J)=ATN(F*RD/DI(J))
209 U(J)=ATN(F*DZ/DY):H(J)=ATN(F*DX/DY):NEXT J
210 FOR J=1 TO N1-1:K=J
220 IF DI(K+1)<=DI(K) THEN 270
230 A=X(K):X(K)=X(K+1):X(K+1)=A:A=Y(K):Y(K)=Y(K+1):Y(K+1)=A
240 A=Z(K):Z(K)=Z(K+1):Z(K+1)=A:A=U(K):U(K)=U(K+1):U(K+1)=A
250 A=H(K):H(K)=H(K+1):H(K+1)=A:A=RS(K):RS(K)=RS(K+1):RS
    (K+1)=A
255 A=DI(K):DI(K)=DI(K+1):DI(K+1)=A
260 K=K-1:IF K>0 THEN 220
270 NEXT J
280 MINU=U(1)-RS(1):MAXU=U(1)+RS(1)
285 MINH=H(1)-RS(1):MAXH=H(1)+RS(1)
290 FOR J=1 TO N1
300 IF U(J)-RS(J)<MINU THEN MINU=U(J)-RS(J)
310 IF U(J)+RS(J)>MAXU THEN MAXU=U(J)+RS(J)
320 IF H(J)-RS(J)<MINH THEN MINH=H(J)-RS(J)
330 IF H(J)+RS(J)>MAXH THEN MAXH=H(J)+RS(J)
340 NEXT J:DH=MAXH-MINH:DU=MAXU-MINU
350 FOR J=1 TO N1
360 H(J)=G*(H(J)-MINH)/DH*WID:U(J)=G*(U(J)-MINU)/DU*HGT
370 RS(J)=G*RS(J)/DH*WID:NEXT J:RETURN
400 REM            PLOT POINTS AND PRINT ON PAPER
405 MU=0:FOR J=1 TO N1:IF U(J)+RS(J)>MU THEN MU=U(J)+RS(J)
406 NEXT J:MU=INT(MU)+1
410 FOR JS=MU TO 0 STEP -1
430 FOR KS=0 TO WID-1:SS=0
440 FOR NS=1 TO N1:PS=SQR((KS-H(NS))^2+(JS-U(NS))^2)
450 IF (PS-RS(NS))<1 THEN SS=1:IF PS<RS(NS) THEN SS=0
460 NEXT NS:PRINT MID$(" *",SS+1,1);:NEXT KS:PRINT:NEXT JS
470 PRINT CHR$(12)
480 RETURN
600 REM            ROTATE POINTS ABOUT AN AXIS
610 FOR J=1 TO N1
620 IF B$="Z" THEN A1=X(J):A2=R(1):A3=Y(J):A4=R(2)
```

```
630 IF B$="Y" THEN A1=X(J):A2=R(1):A3=Z(J):A4=R(3)
640 IF B$="X" THEN A1=Y(J):A2=R(2):A3=Z(J):A4=R(3)
650 P1=A1-A2:P2=A3-A4
660 L=SQR(P1*P1+P2*P2)
670 IF P2=0 THEN A5=-(P1<0)*3.141593
680 IF P1=0 THEN A5=SGN(P2)*1.570796
690 IF P2<>0 AND P1<>0 THEN A5=ATN(P2/P1)-(P1<0)*3.141593
700 A5=A5+E
710 IF B$="Z" THEN X(J)=L*COS(A5)+R(1):Y(J)=L*SIN(A5)+R(2)
720 IF B$="Y" THEN X(J)=L*COS(A5)+R(1):Z(J)=L*SIN(A5)+R(3)
730 IF B$="X" THEN Y(J)=L*COS(A5)+R(2):Z(J)=L*SIN(A5)+R(3)
740 NEXT J:RETURN
READY
```

Lines 10-50 are remark statements stating the nature of the program and giving the credits. Line 60 is a subroutine call to line 100, where the program is set up and the data is read. Line 70 is a call to a subroutine that sorts the points at the centers of the spheres in the order of decreasing distances from a defined viewpoint. This viewpoint could be likened to your eye as it would see the molecule. Line 80 is a subroutine call to line 400, which plots the points and prints them on paper or the video screen. Line 90 is a subroutine call to line 600, which rotates the points about a specified axis. Line 95 is a goto statement that repeats the rotation and printing endlessly. You must interrupt the program to stop it. You might write a loop that would rotate and print out the figures a finite number of times.

Lines 100-195 set variables and arrays and read in data. Line 100 is a remark statement for the section. Line 110 sets E equal to 0.4. E is the rotation increment in radians. N1 is the number of points (spheres) in the figure. RD is the radius of the spheres. F is the perspective factor that makes close objects seem large and far objects seem small. G is the magnification factor. HGT is the height and WID is the width. You may need to adjust the HGT and WID to get a proper figure. Line 120 dimensions the arrays used. X, Y, and Z are the coordinates of the points; V and H are the vertical and horizontal arrays for the positions of the points; RS is the adjusted radius of each sphere; DI is the distance from each point to the viewpoint; R is the point of rotation for each of the axes. Line 130 is a

loop that reads in the X, Y, and Z coordinates. Lines 140-170 contain those values. Line 190 sets R(1) equal to 2.5. R(1) is the point about which the model will rotate when rotating parallel to the X-axis. R(2) is the point that the molecule will rotate about when rotating parallel to the Y-axis and R(3) is the rotation point for the Z-axis, X(0) is the X-value of the viewpoint; Y(0) is the Y-value of the viewpoint and Z(0) is the Z-value for the viewpoint. This is where your eye would be if you were actually viewing the molecule in reality, if that were possible. B$ is a literal string variable that designates the axis of rotation. Changing B$ to "X" or "Y" will allow rotation around the other axes. Line 195 returns control back to line 70.

Lines 200-370 sort the points by their decreasing distances from the coordinates of the viewpoint. Line 210 is a remark statement for the subroutine. Lines 202-209 form a loop which defines DY, the distance from the point to the viewpoint along the Y-axis; DX, the difference between them along the X-axis; and DZ, the difference between them along the Z-axis. If DY is negative the object is behind your head, as it were, and you would have to "back off" by decreasing Y(0). Line 208 defines DI, the distance from the viewpoint to each point. This is the square root of the sum of the differences squared. RS is the adjusted radius for each sphere. In line 209 V and H are the adjusted vertical and horizontal positions for each point.

Lines 210-270 are a modified shell sorting routine that moves the points' coordinates and other associated arrays according to their decreasing distances from the viewpoint. We've seen a sort like this before.

Lines 280 and 285 set the minimum and maximum heights and widths to an arbitrary value, the first one in the array. Lines 290-340 find the actual minimum and maximum values for the height and width values of the points. Line 340 sets DH as the difference in the width and DV as the difference in the height.

Lines 350-370 form a loop that adjusts the values of the points so that they will fill as much of

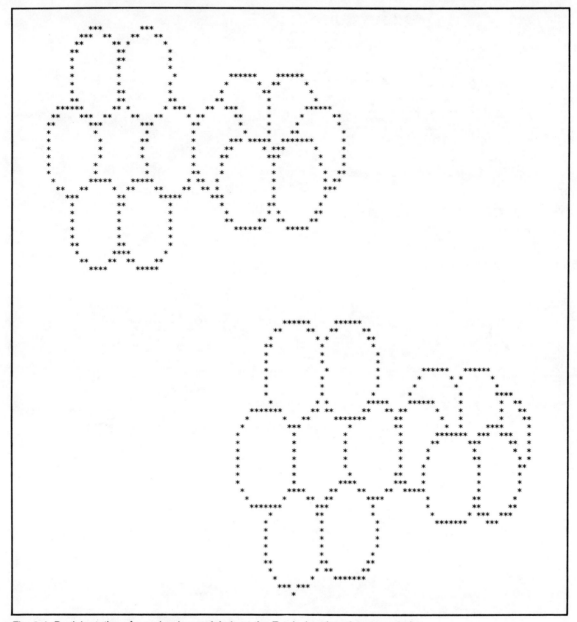

Fig. 3-4. Partial rotation of a molecular model about the Z axis (continued on page 34.)

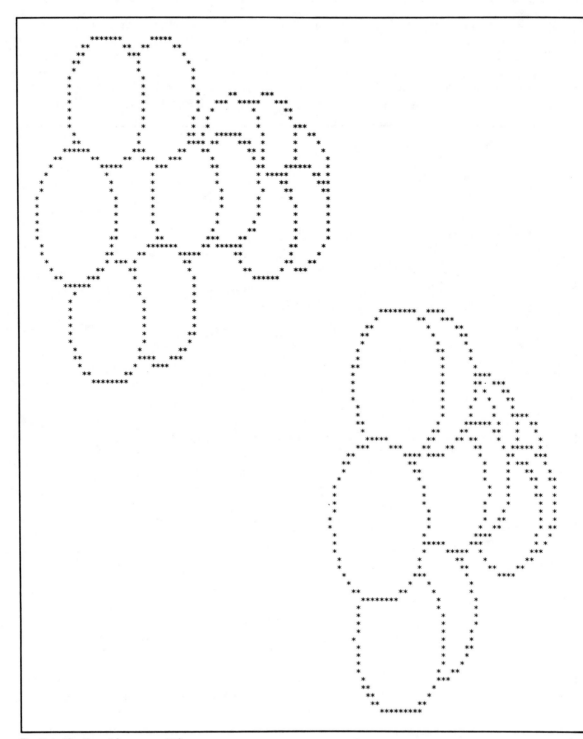

Fig. 3-4. (Continued from page 33.)

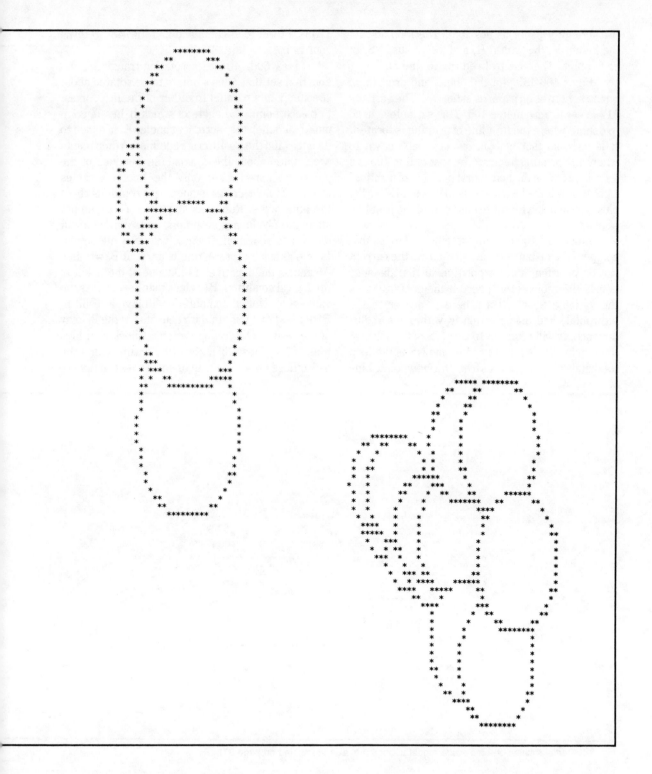

the screen or paper as possible. The loop adjusts the height V, the width, H, and the radius, RS, of each point. Then control returns to line 80.

Lines 400-480 plot the points and print them on the screen or on paper as asterisks. The variable MV is set to zero in line 405. This variable is used to denote where the first line of printing is located. It is used so that we can quickly "tab" down to where the printing begins. The rest of line 405 is a loop used to find the actual first position of printing. Line 406 ends the loop and sets MV as the INT(MV) plus one. We don't want to miss part of the first line of print.

Lines 410-460 contain three nested loops that compute the distance of each point from the current screen position or print position. If that distance equals the radius of a sphere it momentarily sets the variable SS=1. If a sphere is nearer to the viewpoint, and that position is within the radius distance, it will reset SS to zero. JS is the loop for the height, KS is for the width, and NS is the loop for distance of the spheres from the viewpoint. Line

470 is a form feed command and line 480 returns control back to line 90.

Lines 600-740 are a rotation-transformation equation set that allows points to be rotated about specific points parallel to either of the three axes. For each point, the angle of which it lies is computed, and then the increment angle, E, is added to its angle and the position is redefined. When points are rotated about the Z axis, the Z-values of the points do not change; only the X and Y-values change. Similar things happen with rotations about the other axes. Rotations about the Y-axis do not affect the Y-values of the points, and rotations about the X-axis do not affect the X-values of the points. Line 670 has an interesting feature. If P2=0 then A5 equals the negative of the value of the result of the logical condition, P1 is less than zero, times the value of pi. Not all computer's will give a result to PRINT − (2=1) or similar requests for the display of the result of logical operations. Check your system. If P1 is less than zero, the result within the parentheses would be true or equal to − 1. If it were

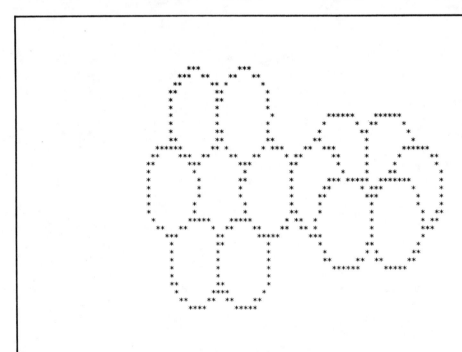

Fig. 3-5. Partial rotation of a molecular model about the Y axis (continued on page 37).

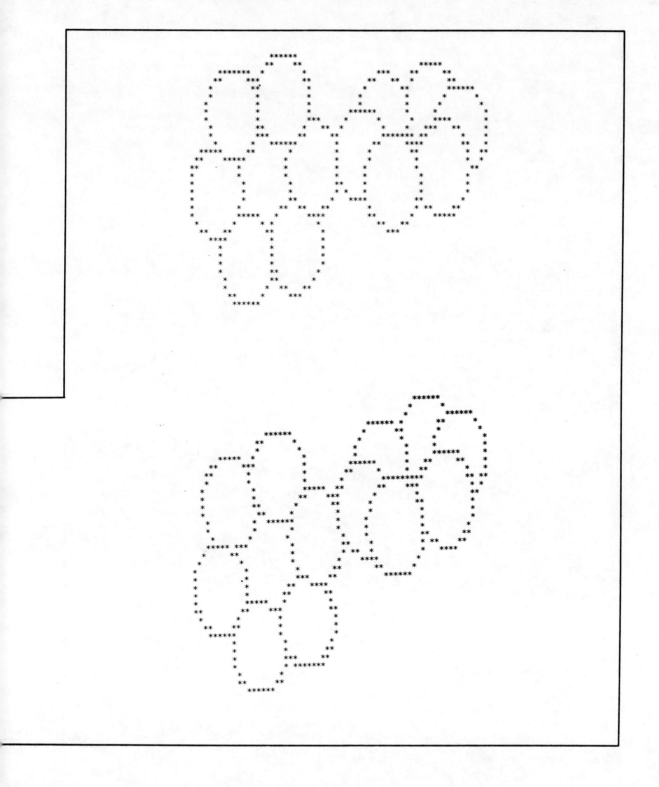

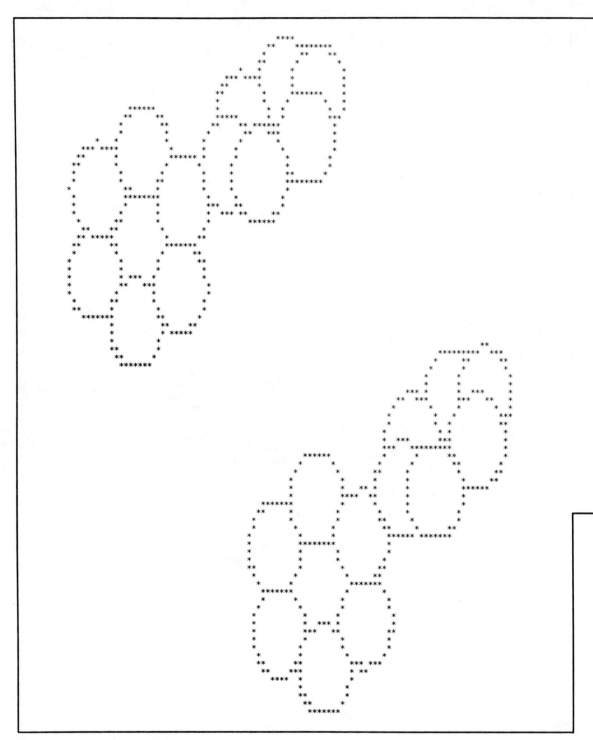

Fig. 3-5. (Continued from page 37.)

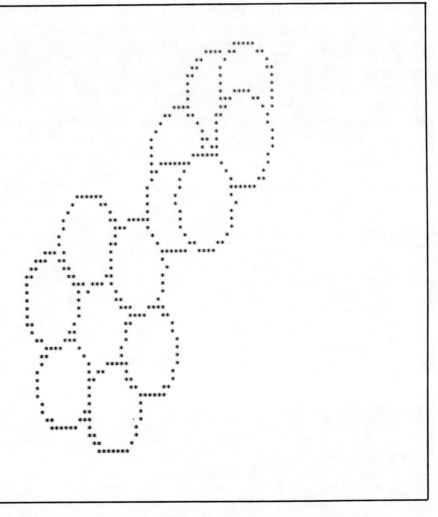

false, it would equal 0. Thus A5 equals Pi if P1 is less than zero, and A5 equals 0 if P1 is not less than zero. A similar type of operation exists in line 690. A5 is the angle (in radians) at which the point lies from the origin, relative to the axis that is involved in the rotation. The increment is added in line 700. The rest of the lines transform the point to the coordinates of its new position after the rotation. Line 740 ends the loop and returns control back to line 95, which repeats the entire process. You may have to finagle a little with the height and width to get the best figure possible.

This low-resolution program really doesn't do justice to what the program is really capable of doing. The next program uses the same data and much of the same programming to make superlative plots.

A High-Resolution Program in BASIC—Program 7

Figure 3-8 shows several partial rotations of the model about the Z-axis. You must admit that the clarity has improved greatly. Figure 3-9 shows the partial rotation about the Y-axis and Figure 3-10 displays a rotation about the X-axis. Figure 3-11 gives the rotation about the X-axis for the six spheres on the left. These figures could be made larger by increasing the HGT and WID variables in the program. Let's look at the program.

```
10 REM          HIGH-RESOLUTION, SPACE-FILLING
20 REM            ROTATING MOLECULAR MODEL
30 REM          WRITTEN BY TIMOTHY J. O'MALLEY
40 REM          COPYRIGHT 1982, TAB BOOKS INC.
50 REM
60 GOSUB 100:REM INITIALIZE PROGRAM AND READ DATA
70 GOSUB 200:REM SORT BY DECREASING DISTANCES TO VIEWPOINT
80 GOSUB 400:REM PLOT POINTS AND PRINT ON PAPER
90 GOSUB 600:REM ROTATE POINTS ABOUT AN AXIS
95 GOTO 70:REM REPEAT ROTATION AND PRINTING INDEFINITELY
100 REM          INITIALIZE PROGRAM AND READ DATA
110 E=0.4:N1=12:RD=0.5:F=0.1:G=0.98:HGT=96:WID=80:W2=80
120 DIM X(N1),Y(N1),Z(N1),U(N1),H(N1),RS(N1),DI(N1),R(3)
130 FOR J=1 TO N1:READ X(J),Y(J),Z(J):NEXT J
140 DATA 0,0,0, 0.5,0,0.87, 1.5,0,0.87, 2,0,0
150 DATA 1.5,0,-0.87, 0.5,0,-0.87, 3,0,0, 3.5,0.348,0.348
160 DATA 4.5,0.348,0.348, 5,0,0, 4.5,-0.348,-0.348
170 DATA 3.5,-0.348,-0.348
180 GOSUB 510:REM SET UP MACHINE LANGUAGE SUBROUTINE FOR
    PRINTER
190 R(1)=2.5:R(2)=0:R(3)=0:X(0)=2.5:Y(0)=-10:Z(0)=1:B$="Z"
195 RETURN
200 REM          SORT BY DECREASING DISTANCES TO VIEWPOINT
202 FOR J=1 TO N1
204 DY=Y(J)-Y(0):IF DY<=0 THEN PRINT"DECREASE Y(0)":STOP
206 DX=X(J)-X(0):DZ=Z(J)-Z(0)
208 DI(J)=SQR(DY*DY+DX*DX+DZ*DZ):RS(J)=ATN(F*RD/DI(J))
209 U(J)=ATN(F*DZ/DY):H(J)=ATN(F*DX/DY):NEXT J
210 FOR J=1 TO N1-1:K=J
220 IF DI(K+1)<=DI(K) THEN 270
230 A=X(K):X(K)=X(K+1):X(K+1)=A:A=Y(K):Y(K)=Y(K+1):Y(K+1)=A
240 A=Z(K):Z(K)=Z(K+1):Z(K+1)=A:A=U(K):U(K)=U(K+1):U(K+1)=A
250 A=H(K):H(K)=H(K+1):H(K+1)=A:A=RS(K):RS(K)=RS(K+1):RS
    (K+1)=A
255 A=DI(K):DI(K)=DI(K+1):DI(K+1)=A
260 K=K-1:IF K>0 THEN 220
270 NEXT J
280 MINU=U(1)-RS(1):MAXU=U(1)+RS(1)
285 MINH=H(1)-RS(1):MAXH=H(1)+RS(1)
290 FOR J=1 TO N1
300 IF U(J)-RS(J)<MINU THEN MINU=U(J)-RS(J)
310 IF U(J)+RS(J)>MAXU THEN MAXU=U(J)+RS(J)
320 IF H(J)-RS(J)<MINH THEN MINH=H(J)-RS(J)
330 IF H(J)+RS(J)>MAXH THEN MAXH=H(J)+RS(J)
340 NEXT J:DH=MAXH-MINH:DU=MAXU-MINU
350 FOR J=1 TO N1
```

```
360 H(J)=G*(H(J)-MINH)/DH*WID:V(J)=G*(V(J)-MINV)/DV*HGT
370 RS(J)=G*RS(J)/DH*WID:NEXT J:RETURN
400 REM          PLOT POINTS AND PRINT ON PAPER
405 MV=0:FOR J=1 TO N1:IF V(J)+RS(J)>MV THEN MV=V(J)+RS(J)
406 NEXT J:MV=INT(MV)+1
410 FOR JS=MV TO 0 STEP -1
420 FOR LS=0 TO 0:GOSUB 490
430 FOR KS=LS*W2 TO LS*W2+W2-1:SS=0
440 FOR NS=1 TO N1:PS=SQR((KS-H(NS))^2+(JS-V(NS))^2)
450 IF (PS-RS(NS))<1 THEN SS=1:IF PS<RS(NS) THEN SS=0
460 NEXT NS:POKE 1,SS:XX=USR(0):NEXT KS,LS
470 POKE 1,13:XX=USR(0):NEXT JS
480 RETURN
490 POKE 1,27:XX=USR(0):POKE 1,75:XX=USR(0):POKE 1,W2
500 XX=USR(0):POKE 1,0:XX=USR(0):RETURN
510 REM      SET UP MACHINE LANGUAGE SUBROUTINE FOR PRINTER
520 POKE 260,0:POKE 261,0:POKE 0,62:POKE 1,27:POKE 2,205
530 POKE 3,12:POKE 4,224:POKE 5,201:XX=USR(0):POKE 1,65
540 XX=USR(0):POKE 1,1:XX=USR(0):RETURN
600 REM            ROTATE POINTS ABOUT AN AXIS
610 FOR J=1 TO N1
620 IF B$="Z" THEN A1=X(J):A2=R(1):A3=Y(J):A4=R(2)
630 IF B$="Y" THEN A1=X(J):A2=R(1):A3=Z(J):A4=R(3)
640 IF B$="X" THEN A1=Y(J):A2=R(2):A3=Z(J):A4=R(3)
650 P1=A1-A2:P2=A3-A4
660 L=SQR(P1*P1+P2*P2)
670 IF P2=0 THEN A5=-(P1<0)*3.141593
680 IF P1=0 THEN A5=SGN(P2)*1.570796
690 IF P2<>0 AND P1<>0 THEN A5=ATN(P2/P1)-(P1<0)*3.141593
700 A5=A5+E
710 IF B$="Z" THEN X(J)=L*COS(A5)+R(1):Y(J)=L*SIN(A5)+R(2)
720 IF B$="Y" THEN X(J)=L*COS(A5)+R(1):Z(J)=L*SIN(A5)+R(3)
730 IF B$="X" THEN Y(J)=L*COS(A5)+R(2):Z(J)=L*SIN(A5)+R(3)
740 NEXT J:RETURN
READY
```

The two programs are the same except for several lines. Line 10 says "high-resolution" instead of "low-resolution." In line 100 we've added the variable W2 and have increased the values of HGT and WID. We have added line 180 which sets up the machine language subroutine for passing numbers to the printer, bypassing the BASIC operating system. Again, we could change that subroutine to BASIC statements. We have also added line 420, which is a nested loop that sets up the

configuration for the printer to accept numbers and print them as graphics. Line 430 has been changed, as has line 460. Line 470 is also different. Lines 490-540 are the same kind of instructions as we saw for the high-resolution function plotter earlier. The rest of this program is the same as the low-resolution version.

By changing N1 you can read in more data and plot more spheres. You can increase the height and width of the plotting area by changing WID and

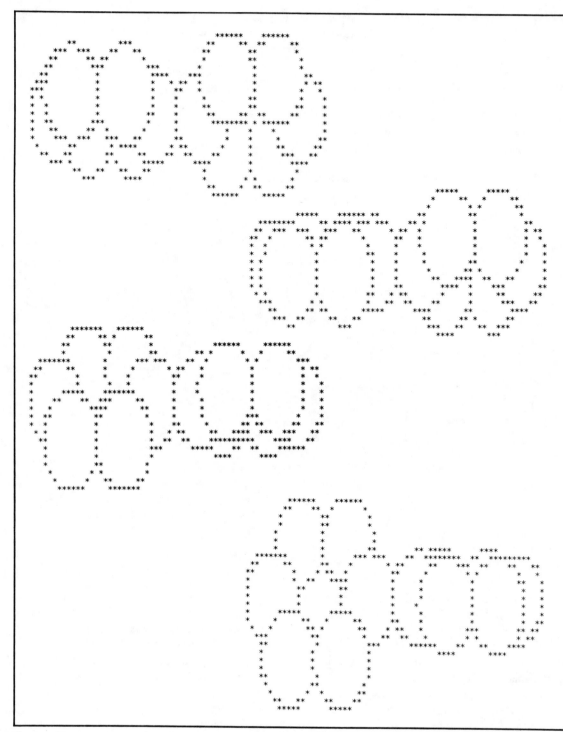

Fig. 3-6. Partial rotation of a molecular model about the X axis.

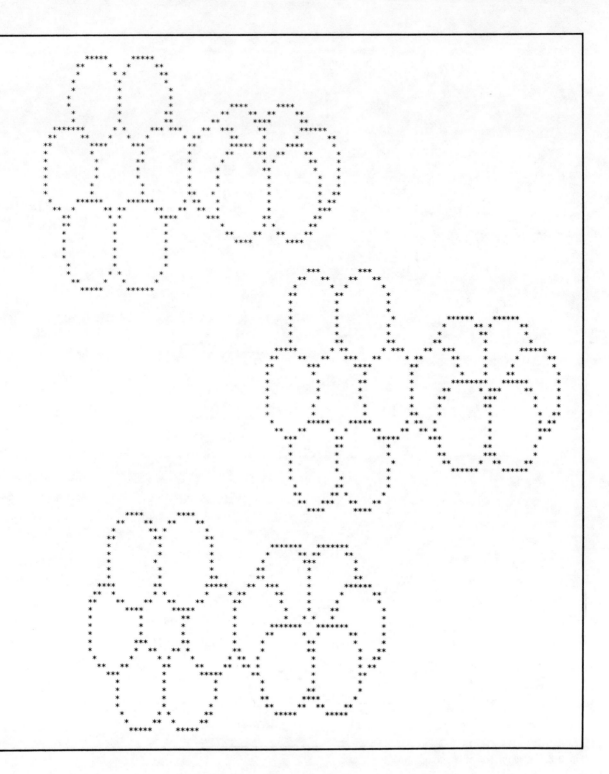

Fig. 3-7. Partial rotation of left group about the X axis.

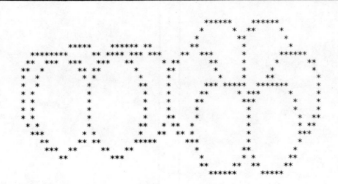

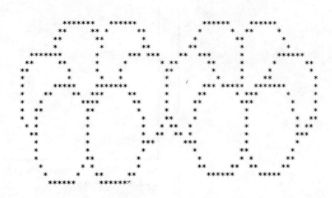

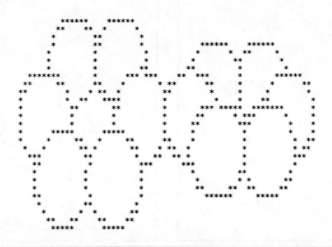

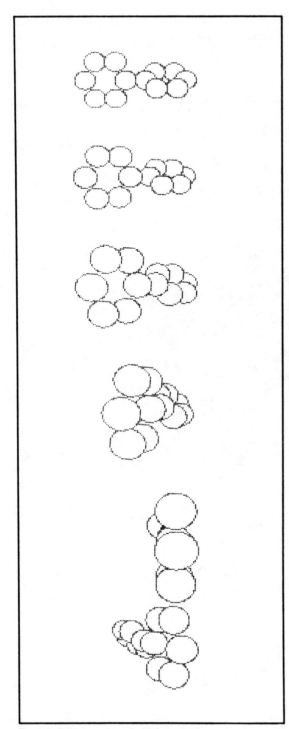

Fig. 3-8. Partial rotation of a high-resolution molecular model about the Z axis.

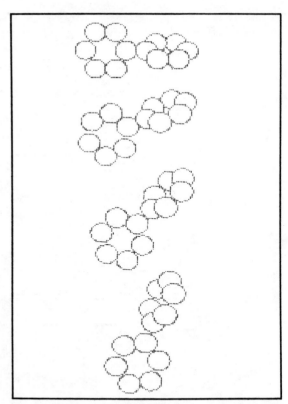

Fig. 3-9. Partial rotation of a high-resolution molecular model about the Y axis.

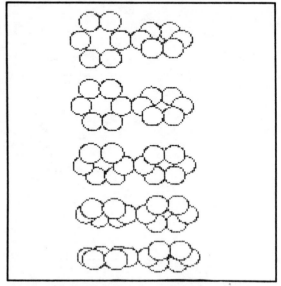

Fig. 3-10. Partial rotation of a high-resolution molecular model about the X axis.

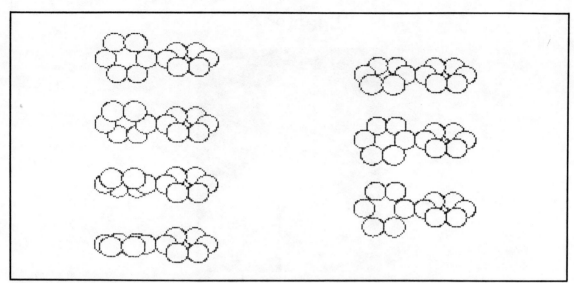

Fig. 3-11. Partial rotation of the left group of the high-resolution model about the X axis.

HGT. If you want to show different kinds of atoms in the molecular model you might read in different radii for them with data statements. All the spheres in our model had the same actual radius, although they looked larger when they were closer to the viewpoint. You might even change line 450 to randomly shade the spheres. We could spend a lot of time with this program, but let's go on to bigger and better things. It doesn't pay to stay in one place too long.

Chapter 4

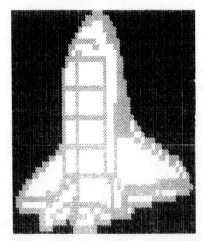

Three-Dimensional Perspective

We briefly discussed perspective when we plotted a three-dimensional figure. We learned a little bit about erasing hidden points both in the function plotters and in the molecular model. This chapter deals with the drawing of figures that have straight lines and are in perspective. We will see all the lines at once, giving the figures the appearance of wire models.

THE NATURE OF PERSPECTIVE

What is it about sight that makes distant objects appear small and close objects appear large and that makes tall buildings seem to shrink down toward the horizon? The answer lies with geometry and trigonometry. Distances twice as great, make objects seem one-half as large. When our eyes are very close to objects, that object appears very large and vice versa. The angle between the top of the object, our eye, and the bottom of the object decreases with distance. The same is true for the width. Although we have not really answered the question, we have enough information now to write computer programs that draw perspective line drawings.

Perspective Plotting

In Chapter 3 we mentioned a couple of equations that we used to plot points in perspective. They contained some numbers that we had to define rather arbitrarily. We will now talk about them further and discuss how to draw perspective lines.

Let's look at those equations. They were: V=F1* ATN(F2*DZ/DY) and H=F1*(F2* DX/DY), although in the programs we used the variables, G and F, for F1 and F2, respectively. We actually used two steps. We set V=ATN(F*DZ/DY); then adjusted it to fill the screen, and then readjusted it using the G factor. In these equations G or F1 is the magnification factor, and F or F2 is equal to the inverse of the distance that we set as one-half infinity to the eye. In other words if we were using a vanishing point type of perspective drawing, this would be equal to one-half the distance to the vanishing point on the paper. It's a fudge factor, really. The F1 factor is for the scaling of the figure and the F2 factor is for the apparent distortion in size as an object approaches very close. If we increase the value of F1, the figure will be magnified. If we increase the value of F2, it really becomes distorted, much as if it were viewed through a fisheye lens.

In the equations, V is the plotted vertical position of the point on the screen or paper, and H is the horizontal position of the point. DX is the difference, along the X dimension, between the coordinate of the point and the X-coordinate of the viewpoint. DY is the difference between the Y-coordinate of the point and the viewpoint, and DZ is the difference between the Z-coordinate of the point and the viewpoint. ATN is the arctangent function.

What we do in the perspective line drawings is to find the V and H and construct a linear line connecting them. We make the assumption that all the points on a straight line between two perspective points are in perspective also. I offer no mathematical proof; we must rely on an intuitive feeling that the assumption is true.

PERSPECTIVE LINE PLOTTERS IN BASIC

We will look at two perspective line plotters; one is low-resolution and one is high-resolution. The low-resolution plotter will be used to draw some simple solid geometric shapes, and the high-resolution one will be used to draw the perspective lines of a house.

Low-Resolution Program In BASIC—Program 8

Figure 4-1 shows solid geometric forms as they are rotated about the vertical axis. The objects are supposed to be a pyramid on a square base, a cube, and two flat diamonds. The low resolution really does not do justice to the program, which will be modified to create a high-resolution drawing of a house.

```
10 REM                LOW-RESOLUTION LINE PLOTTER
20 REM             WRITTEN BY TIMOTHY J. O'MALLEY
30 REM             COPYRIGHT 1982, TAB BOOKS INC.
40 REM
50 GOSUB 300:REM     INITIALIZE VARIABLES
70 FOR J=0 TO U:FOR K=0 TO W:VA(J,K)=32:NEXT K,J
75 GOSUB 600:REM     ROTATE POINTS ABOUT AXIS
80 GOSUB 800:REM     TRANSLATE X,Y,Z TO H,V
100 GOSUB 1200:REM   DRAW LINES CONNECTING POINTS
105 GOSUB 1600:REM PRINT OUT LOW RESOLUTION
110 GOTO 70
300 REM                INITIALIZE VARIABLES
305 IP=21:IA=43
310 DIM I(IA),X(IP),Y(IP),Z(IP),R(3),V(IP),H(IP)
320 FOR J=1 TO IP
330 READ X(J),Y(J),Z(J)
340 NEXT J
345 DATA 0,0,1, 1,0,1, 1,0,0, 0,0,0, 0,1,1
346 DATA 1,1,1, 1,1,0, 0,1,0, 2,2,0, 3,2,0
347 DATA 3,3,0, 2,3,0, 2.5,2.5,1
348 DATA 3,0,1, 2.5,0,0.5, 3,0,0, 3.5,0,0.5
349 DATA 0,3,0, 0,3.5,0.5, 0,3,1, 0,2.5,0.5
380 FOR J=1 TO IA
```

```
390 READ I(J)
400 NEXT J
405 DATA 1,2,3,4,1,5,6,7,8,5,0,4,8,0,2,6,0,3,7,0
410 DATA 9,10,11,12,9,13,10,0,11,13,12,0
415 DATA 14,15,16,17,14,0
416 DATA 18,19,20,21,18
420 R(1)=2:R(2)=2:R(3)=0.5
430 X(0)=2:Y(0)=-10:Z(0)=3
440 F=0.1:G=1:REM F IS THE DISTORTION AND G IS MAGNIFICATION.
450 S=1:T=IP
460 B$="Z"
470 W=63:U=63
475 DIM VA(U,W)
480 E=0.4:REM ROTATION INCREMENT
500 RETURN
600 REM                     ROTATE POINTS ABOUT AXIS
610 FOR J=S TO T
620 IF B$="Z" THEN A1=X(J):A2=R(1):A3=Y(J):A4=R(2)
630 IF B$="Y" THEN A1=X(J):A2=R(1):A3=Z(J):A4=R(3)
640 IF B$="X" THEN A1=Y(J):A2=R(2):A3=Z(J):A4=R(3)
650 P1=A1-A2:P2=A3-A4
660 L=SQR(P1*P1+P2*P2)
670 IF P2=0 THEN A5=0-(P1<0)*3.141593
680 IF P1=0 THEN A5=SGN(P2)*1.570796
690 IF P2<>0 AND P1<>0 THEN A5=ATN(P2/P1)-(P1<0)*3.141593
700 A5=A5+E
710 IF B$="Z" THEN X(J)=L*COS(A5)+R(1):Y(J)=L*SIN(A5)+R(2)
720 IF B$="Y" THEN X(J)=L*COS(A5)+R(1):Z(J)=L*SIN(A5)+R(3)
730 IF B$="X" THEN Y(J)=L*COS(A5)+R(2):Z(J)=L*SIN(A5)+R(3)
740 NEXT J
750 RETURN
800 REM                     TRANSLATE X,Y,Z TO H,V
810 FOR J=1 TO IP
820 DY=Y(J)-Y(0):IF DY<=0 THEN PRINT "DECREASE Y(0)":STOP
830 DX=X(J)-X(0)
840 DZ=Z(J)-Z(0)
850 V(J)=ATN(F*DZ/DY):REM VERTICAL SCREEN POSITION
860 H(J)=ATN(F*DX/DY):REM HORIZONTAL SCREEN POSITION
870 NEXT J
880 MINV=V(1):MAXV=V(1)
890 MINH=H(1):MAXH=H(1)
900 FOR J=1 TO IP
910 IF V(J)<MINV THEN MINV=V(J)
920 IF V(J)>MAXV THEN MAXV=V(J)
930 IF H(J)<MINH THEN MINH=H(J)
940 IF H(J)>MAXH THEN MAXH=H(J)
```

```
950 NEXT J
960 DH=MAXH-MINH
970 DV=MAXV-MINV
980 FOR J=1 TO IP
990 H(J)=G*(H(J)-MINH)/DH*W
1000 V(J)=G*(V(J)-MINV)/DV*U
1110 NEXT J
1120 RETURN
1200 REM                DRAW LINES CONNECTING POINTS
1210 FOR J=1 TO IA-1
1220 IF I(J)=0 OR I(J+1)=0 THEN 1340
1230 HH=H(I(J+1))-H(I(J))
1240 VV=V(I(J+1))-V(I(J))
1250 SN=SGN(HH)
1260 IF SN=0 THEN 1360
1270 M=VV/HH
1280 B=V(I(J))-M*H(I(J))
1290 SP=SQR(VV*VV+HH*HH)
1300 FOR K=H(I(J)) TO H(I(J+1)) STEP HH/SP
1310 P=M*K+B
1320 GOSUB 1500
1330 NEXT K
1340 NEXT J
1350 RETURN
1360 REM                SLOPE EQUALS INFINITY
1370 K=H(I(J))
1380 IF SGN(VV)=0 THEN P=H(I(J)):GOSUB 1500:GOTO 1340
1390 FOR P=V(I(J)) TO V(I(J+1)) STEP SGN(VV)
1400 GOSUB 1500
1410 NEXT P
1420 GOTO 1340
1500 REM          PLOTTING SUBROUTINE
1510 IF P>U OR P<0 OR K>W OR K<0 THEN RETURN
1520 V1=INT(P):V2=INT(K)
1530 VA(V1,V2)=42
1540 RETURN
1600 REM                LOW RESOLUTION PRINTER
1605 MH=0:FOR NM=1 TO IP:IF MH<V(NM) THEN MH=V(NM)
1607 NEXT NM:MH=INT(MH)+1
1610 FOR JS=MH TO 0 STEP -1:FOR KS=0 TO W
1630 PRINT CHR$(VA(JS,KS));:NEXT KS:PRINT
1660 NEXT JS:PRINT CHR$(12);:RETURN
READY
```

Let's look at this program line by line. Lines 10-40 are remarks about the nature of the program.

Line 50 is a subroutine call to line 300, which sets up the program by reading data, defining variables

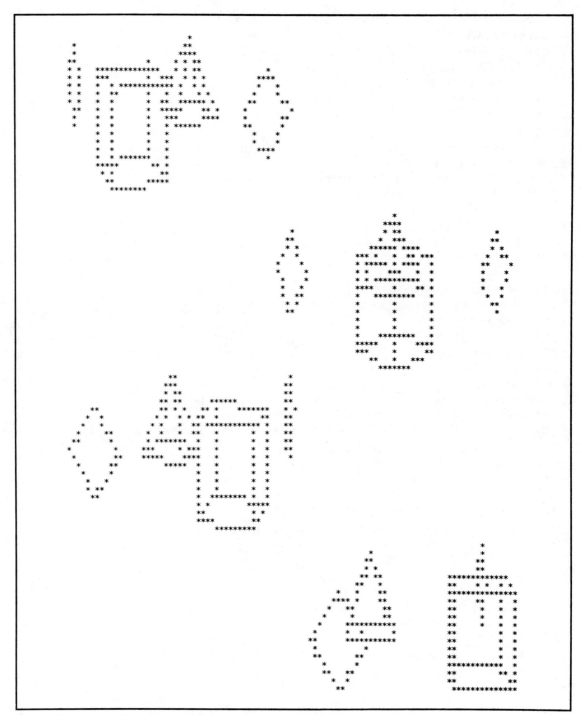

Fig. 4-1. Partial rotation of solid geometric forms about the vertical axis.

and dimensioning arrays. Line 70 is a nested loop that sets all the elements of the VA array equal to 32. 32 is the ASCII code for a blank space. Line 75 is a subroutine call to line 600, which rotates points about an axis. Line 80 is a call to line 800, which translates the X, Y, and Z coordinates of each point to a horizontal and vertical value so that it can be stored in the array, VA. Line 100 calls the subroutine at 1200, which draws lines between points, and line 105 prints out the low-resolution figures as asterisks. Line 110 goes to line 70 to repeat the rotation and printing without end. You might want to change it to a finite number of repetitions, possibly by using a loop.

Line 300 is a remark statement for the initialization of the program. In line 305, IP is the number of points that we give coordinates for. These points are corners in the figure. IA contains the number of points in the I array. This controls which points are connected to which points. Line 310 dimensions various arrays used in the program. Lines 320-340 read the coordinates of the points, these coordinates are found in lines 345-349. Lines 380-400 form a loop that reads in the I array elements from data statements in lines 405-416. Point 1 is connected to point 2, which is connected to point 3, which is connected to point 4, which is connected back to point 1, which is also connected to point 5, and so forth. A 0 is used as a terminator for the line connections. By using this scheme, the computer will be able to compute the points for the connecting lines and thus determine where the lines are to be made. Line 420 says that the X-axis rotations are to be made about the line $X=2$; Y-axis rotations about the line $Y=2$ and Z-axis rotations about the line $Z=0.5$. In line 430 the coordinates of the viewpoint are defined. Line 440 sets the perspective factors. In line 450, S is the index of the first point to be rotated and T is the index of the last point to be rotated. In this case, we want to rotate all of them. Using these variables allow greater flexibility for the rotations. Line 460 says to rotate the points about the Z axis. Line 470 contains the variables for the width and height respectively. Line 475 dimensions the VA array, which will store

the points and lines of the figures. Line 480 defines the rotation increment. Line 500 returns control to line 70.

Lines 600-750 rotate points using the same set of transformation equations that we have seen before. Line 610 allows you to rotate only some of the points, those from index S to index T. It then returns control to line 80. Lines 800-1120 form a subroutine that translates the three-dimensional points to two-dimensional positions in the arrays H and V. We have examined this subroutine before, so enough said about it. Line 1120 returns control to line 100.

Lines 1200-1350 draw lines connecting the points indicated in array I. If two points have the same vertical position the short subroutine in lines 1360-1420 is used. The subroutine is necessary because the program defines the equation of the slope of the line between the two points and a vertical line has an infinite slope. Line 1220 checks for the zero, indicating the terminus of a line connection. Lines 1230-1240 find the difference between the horizontal and vertical positions of the points so that the slope, M, can be calculated in line 1270. Line 1280 computes B, the Y-intercept, so that the equation of the current line can be computed in line 1310 of the program. SP, in line 1290, is the distance between the two points. Lines 1300-1330 fill the space between the two points with an appropriate number of other points, making a line.

The plotting subroutine in lines 1500-1540 is called by the line connecting subroutine. This subroutine checks to see whether or not the points are outside of the dimensions of the array by using the if statement in line 1510. If they are not, it rounds the position of the point to integers in line 1520 and sets the VA array at that position to 42. 42 is the ASCII code for the asterisk. You may change this number if you want to print a different symbol.

Lines 1600-1660 form the low-resolution printer routine. The variable MH is used as the row number in the array where the printing should start. This way we eliminate the printing of a lot of empty spaces at the top of the array. As I said before, it is a "tab" of sorts. The loop starting in 1610 simply prints out the CHR$ of each of the elements in the array. Line 1660 contains a statement that clears the screen because it is a form feed command.

That concludes the program. Now we will look at a program that uses much the same programming to produce a line drawing of a house.

High-Resolution Program In BASIC—Program 9

Figure 4-2 depicts a few of the possible views of the house produced by the high-resolution line drawing program. When using line drawings, it is best to use as few lines as possible or else the figure will appear cluttered and confusing. Let's examine the program listing.

```
10 REM            PERSPECTIVE LINE PLOTTER OF HOUSE
20 REM             WRITTEN BY TIMOTHY J. O'MALLEY
30 REM            COPYRIGHT 1982, TAB BOOKS INC.
40 REM
50 GOSUB 300:REM       INITIALIZE VARIABLES
70 FOR J=0 TO U:FOR K=0 TO W:VA(J,K)=0:NEXT K,J
75 GOSUB 600:REM       ROTATE POINTS ABOUT AXIS
80 GOSUB 800:REM       TRANSLATE X,Y,Z TO H,V
100 GOSUB 1200:REM   DRAW LINES CONNECTING POINTS
105 GOSUB 1600:REM      PRINT OUT HIGH RESOLUTION
110 GOTO 70
300 REM               INITIALIZE VARIABLES
305 IP=34:IA=87
310 DIM I(IA),X(IP),Y(IP),Z(IP),R(3),V(IP),H(IP)
320 FOR J=1 TO IP
330 READ X(J),Y(J),Z(J)
340 NEXT J
345 DATA 0,0,0, 0,48,0, 36,48,0, 36,18,0, 20,18,0
346 DATA 20,0,0, 20,0,10, 0,0,10, 0,8,10, 20,8,10
347 DATA 10,8,12, 0,8,20, 10,8,27, 20,8,20,0,40,20
348 DATA 10,40,27, 20,40,20, 10,34,27, 20,28,20,28,34,27
349 DATA 20,48,20, 28,48,27, 36,48,20, 36,28,20,28,28,27
350 DATA 20,28,12, 36,28,12, 36,18,10, 20,18,10
351 DATA 20,48,0, 20,40,12, 20,48,10,0,48,10, 0,40,12
380 FOR J=1 TO IA
390 READ I(J)
400 NEXT J
405 DATA 1,2,3,4,5,6,1,8,7,10,9,8,11,7,6,0,9,12,13,14,10,0
410 DATA 12,15,16,13,0,17,18,19,20,17,0,18,20,0
415 DATA 19,25,24,23,22,21,17,0,25,22,0
416 DATA 23,3,0,24,27,26,19,0,26,29,5,0,29,28,27,0,28,4,0
417 DATA 21,30,0,33,34,31,32,33,2,0,17,31,0,15,34
418 DATA 0,16,17,0,14,19
420 R(1)=18:R(2)=24:R(3)=14
430 X(0)=6:Y(0)=-100:Z(0)=6
440 F=0.1:G=1:REM F IS THE DISTORTION AND G IS MAGNIFICATION.
450 S=1:T=IP
460 B$="Z"
```

```
470 W=253:U=25:W2=127
475 DIM VA(U,W)
480 E=0.4:REM ROTATION INCREMENT
490 POKE 260,0:POKE 261,0:POKE 0,62:POKE 1,27:POKE 2,205
500 POKE 3,12:POKE 4,224:POKE 5,201:XX=USR(0):POKE 1,65
510 XX=USR(0):POKE 1,1:XX=USR(0):RETURN
600 REM                 ROTATE POINTS ABOUT AXIS
610 FOR J=S TO T
620 IF B$="Z" THEN A1=X(J):A2=R(1):A3=Y(J):A4=R(2)
630 IF B$="Y" THEN A1=X(J):A2=R(1):A3=Z(J):A4=R(3)
640 IF B$="X" THEN A1=Y(J):A2=R(2):A3=Z(J):A4=R(3)
650 P1=A1-A2:P2=A3-A4
660 L=SQR(P1*P1+P2*P2)
670 IF P2=0 THEN A5=0-(P1<0)*3.141593
680 IF P1=0 THEN A5=SGN(P2)*1.570796
690 IF P2<>0 AND P1<>0 THEN A5=ATN(P2/P1)-(P1<0)*3.141593
700 A5=A5+E
710 IF B$="Z" THEN X(J)=L*COS(A5)+R(1):Y(J)=L*SIN(A5)+R(2)
720 IF B$="Y" THEN X(J)=L*COS(A5)+R(1):Z(J)=L*SIN(A5)+R(3)
730 IF B$="X" THEN Y(J)=L*COS(A5)+R(2):Z(J)=L*SIN(A5)+R(3)
740 NEXT J
750 RETURN
800 REM               TRANSLATE X,Y,Z TO H,V
810 FOR J=1 TO IP
820 DY=Y(J)-Y(0):IF DY<=0 THEN PRINT "DECREASE Y(0)":STOP
830 DX=X(J)-X(0)
840 DZ=Z(J)-Z(0)
850 V(J)=ATN(F*DZ/DY):REM VERTICAL SCREEN POSITION
860 H(J)=ATN(F*DX/DY):REM HORIZONTAL SCREEN POSITION
870 NEXT J
880 MINV=V(1):MAXV=V(1)
890 MINH=H(1):MAXH=H(1)
900 FOR J=1 TO IP
910 IF V(J)<MINV THEN MINV=V(J)
920 IF V(J)>MAXV THEN MAXV=V(J)
930 IF H(J)<MINH THEN MINH=H(J)
940 IF H(J)>MAXH THEN MAXH=H(J)
950 NEXT J
960 DH=MAXH-MINH
970 DV=MAXV-MINV
980 FOR J=1 TO IP
990 H(J)=G*(H(J)-MINH)/DH*W
1000 V(J)=G*(V(J)-MINV)/DV*U
1110 NEXT J
1120 RETURN
1200 REM                  DRAW LINES CONNECTING POINTS
```

```
1210 FOR J=1 TO IA-1
1220 IF I(J)=0 OR I(J+1)=0 THEN 1340
1230 HH=H(I(J+1))-H(I(J))
1240 VV=V(I(J+1))-V(I(J))
1250 SN=SGN(HH)
1260 IF SN=0 THEN 1360
1270 M=VV/HH
1280 B=V(I(J))-M*H(I(J))
1290 SP=SQR(VV*VV+HH*HH)
1300 FOR K=H(I(J)) TO H(I(J+1)) STEP HH/SP
1310 P=M*K+B
1320 GOSUB 1500
1330 NEXT K
1340 NEXT J
1350 RETURN
1360 REM                    SLOPE EQUALS INFINITY
1370 K=H(I(J))
1380 IF SGN(VV)=0 THEN P=H(I(J)):GOSUB 1500:GOTO 1340
1390 FOR P=V(I(J)) TO V(I(J+1)) STEP SGN(VV)/12
1400 GOSUB 1500
1410 NEXT P
1420 GOTO 1340
1500 REM          PLOTTING SUBROUTINE
1510 IF P>U OR P<0 OR K>W OR K<0 THEN RETURN
1520 V1=INT(P):V2=INT(K)
1530 VA(V1,V2)=VA(V1,V2)OR2^INT(12*(P-V1))
1540 RETURN
1600 REM                    HIGH RESOLUTION PRINTER
1610 FOR JS=U TO 0 STEP -1:FOR MS=11 TO 0 STEP -1
1620 BS=INT(2^MS):FOR LS=0 TO 1:GOSUB 1650
1630 FOR KS=LS*W2 TO LS*W2+W2-1:POKE 1,SGN(BS AND VA(JS,KS))
1640 XX=USR(0):NEXT KS,LS:POKE 1,13:XX=USR(0):NEXT MS,JS
1645 POKE 1,12:XX=USR(0):RETURN
1650 POKE 1,27:XX=USR(0):POKE 1,75:XX=USR(0):POKE 1,W2
1660 XX=USR(0):POKE 1,0:XX=USR(0):RETURN
READY
```

Lines 10-40 are remark statements for the program. Lines 50-110 are the same as they were in the last program, except that now the subroutine at line 1600 prints out figures in high-resolution. Line 70 sets the elements of the array to zero rather than 32 since we are using a different method to print out points. Line 305 sets IP and IA at larger values because there are more points and connections. We have added a few more data statements to include this information. We have changed line 420 to rotate the figure about different axes than we did in the last program. Line 430 is also different. In line 470, we added the variable W2 and altered the values of W and U. We have added the statements in lines 490-510 to set up a machine-language subroutine to pass numbers directly to the printer as we have done in other programs.

The translating subroutine is exactly as it was

before. The line connecting subroutine is the same except for line 1390, which divides the step SGN(VV), by 12. Line 1530 does a Boolean algebra binary-logical OR on the numbers in VA(V1,V2) using 2 to the power of the integer of 12 times P minus V1. In this program we are actually plotting bits of numbers when we plot the figure.

The high-resolution printer is very different from the low-resolution printer. Therefore we have added a nested loop, MS, to take care of the bits of the numbers. It's much like the high-resolution printer routine that we used in the program that created a three-dimensional plot of a function.

ROTATING POINTS IN SPACE

We've seen programs that are rotation transformation equations, but we really have not discussed how we arrived at the equations. Neither have we discussed how to rotate points about an arbitrary axis. We will do both in this section.

Rotation About a Defined Axis

We can rotate a set of points parallel to the X, Y or Z-axis, although the rotation doesn't have to be about the axis itself. We can designate R(1) to be the point about which the points are rotated when we perform an X-axis rotation; for example, if R(1)=3, we are rotating about the line X=3. R(2) is for the Y-axis and R(3) is for the Z-axis.

If we rotate points about the X-axis, the X-coordinate of each point does not change. As a point is rotated, it circumscribes a plane. The locus of the points is a circle on that plane. The other two coordinates do change, however. As we rotate about the X-axis, the Y-coordinate changes as a function of the cosine of its original angle plus the increment of rotation. The Z-coordinate changes as a function of the sine of its original angle plus the rotation increment. In the programs that include rotations, we have generalized the set of equations

so that A1 is the first coordinate that changes and A2 is the second. We must find the size of the angle that each point is rotationally displaced about its axis. Then we must add the increment to that angle and redefine the points to get the rotation.

Rotation About an Arbitrary Axis

What if we wanted to rotate a set of points about an arbitrary axis, one that isn't parallel to any of the three axes? One solution is to rotate the set of points parallel to an axis first, then perform the rotation that you want, and finally rotate the points back from the parallel axis to the original position. The result would be that the points would seem to rotate only about the arbitrary axis. Another solution is to redefine our transformation equations to include rotation about an arbitrary axis. In the programs that follow, we will rotate some points about an arbitrary axis using the first method.

INTERACTIVE SPACE SHUTTLE SIMULATIONS IN BASIC

We now look at two versions of a space shuttle program in BASIC; one is a low-resolution version and one is a high-resolution version. We will be able to manipulate the model in three dimensions and operate the cargo bay doors.

A Low-Resolution Perspective Line Program—Program 10

This first program uses block-type graphics to make a figure. Figure 4-3 shows the model of the space shuttle as it may look on the video screen when the program starts. Figure 4-4 shows the result of rotating the model along the X-axis 1.0 radians. These figures show the wings, tail, cargo bay doors, nose and windows of the spacecraft. By adding more points and lines, you could embellish the figures; however, in low-resolution they might look too jumbled.

```
10 REM          LOW-RESOLUTION SPACE SHUTTLE SIMULATION
20 REM              WRITTEN BY TIMOTHY J. O'MALLEY
30 REM              COPYRIGHT 1982, TAB BOOKS INC.
35 REM
40 PRINT CHR$(12);
```

```
41 PRINT:PRINT:PRINT
42 PRINT TAB(15);"INTERACTIVE SPACE SHUTTLE SIMULATION"
43 PRINT TAB(18);"WRITTEN BY TIMOTHY J. O'MALLEY"
44 PRINT TAB(18);"COPYRIGHT 1982, TAB BOOKS INC."
45 PRINT:PRINT:PRINT
46 INPUT "DO YOU WANT INSTRUCTIONS (YES OR NO)";AN$
47 IF AN$="YES" THEN GOSUB 2000
48 PRINT:PRINT:PRINT
49 PRINT "THE COMPUTER WILL NOW SET UP THE PROGRAM."
50 GOSUB 3000:REM    DEFINE BLOCK GRAPHICS
60 GOSUB 300:REM     INITIALIZE VARIABLES
65 GOSUB 500:GOSUB 800:GOSUB 1200:REM DISPLAY START
70 INPUT "COMMAND";CM$
75 M1$=LEFT$(CM$,1):E=VAL(RIGHT$(CM$,(LEN(CM$)-2)))
80 GOSUB 4000:REM    INTERPRET COMMANDS
90 GOSUB 6000:REM THIS LINE IS OPTIONAL
100 GOTO 70
300 REM                INITIALIZE VARIABLES
305 IP=112:IA=187:PTR=0:ID=0
310 DIM I(IA),X(IP),Y(IP),Z(IP),R(3),V(IP),H(IP)
315 DIM STL(100)
316 DIM SX(IP),SY(IP),SZ(IP)
318 DIM SN(100)
320 FOR J=1 TO IP
330 READ X(J),Y(J),Z(J)
335 SX(J)=X(J):SY(J)=Y(J):SZ(J)=Z(J)
340 NEXT J
345 DATA 0,0,0, 0,3.75,1, 0,6.5,3.75, 0,7.5,7.5
346 DATA 0,6.5,11.25, 0,3.5,14, 0,0,15, 0,-3.75,14
347 DATA 0,-6.5,11.25, 0,-7.5,7.5, 0,-6.5,3.75,0,-3.75,1
348 DATA 60,0,0, 60,3.75,1,60,6.5,3.75,60,7.5,7.5
349 DATA 60,6.5,11.25,60,3.75,14,60,0,15,60,-3.75,14
350 DATA 60,-6.5,11.25,60,-7.5,7.5,60,-6.5,3.75,60,-3.75,1
351 DATA 0,0,15,0,-3.75,14,0,-6.5,11.25,0,-7.5,7.5
352 DATA 60,0,15,60,-3.75,14,60,-6.5,11.25,60,-7.5,7.5
353 DATA 0,0,15,0,3.75,14,0,6.5,11.25,0,7.5,7.5
354 DATA 60,0,15,60,3.75,14,60,6.5,11.25,60,7.5,7.5
355 DATA 62,0,15,77,0,45,87,0,42.5,82,0,20
356 DATA 77,0,15,77,0,20,85,0,40.5,86,0,40.5
357 DATA 0,-7.5,0,31,-14.5,0,39,-17,0,60,-37,0,66,-40,0
358 DATA 76,-42,0,79.5,-28,0,83,-13,0,93,-9,0,93,9,0
359 DATA 83,13,0,79.5,28,0,76,42,0,66,40,0,60,37,0
360 DATA 39,17,0,31,14.5,0,0,7.5,0,41.5,-15,0,63,-38,0
361 DATA 69,-40,0,72,-41,0,74,-28,0,77,-13,0,71,-13,0
362 DATA 41.5,15,0,63,38,0,69,40,0,72,41,0,74,28,0
363 DATA 77,13,0, 71,13,0, 30,7.5,7.5
```

```
364 DATA  -28,0,4,-24,0,8,-24,-2,7.5,-24,-3.5,6,-24,-4,4
365 DATA  -24,-3.5,2,-24,-2,.5,-24,0,0,-24,2,.5,-24,3.5,2
366 DATA  -24,4,4,-24,3.5,6,-24,2,7.5,-6.5,-6,14.5
367 DATA  -9,-6,14.5,-10,-3,14.5,-9,-3,15,-9,3,15
368 DATA  -10,3,14.5,-9,6,14.5,-6.5,6,14.5,-6.5,7.5,13
369 DATA  -10,7.5,12,-11.5,3.5,13,-12.5,1,13,-10,1.5,14.5
370 DATA  -12.5,-1,13,-10,-1.5,14.5,-11.5,-3.5,13
371 DATA  -10,-7.5,12,-6.5,-7.5,13
380 FOR J=1 TO IA
390 READ I(J)
400 NEXT J
405 DATA  1,2,3,4,5,6,7,8,9,10,11,12,1,0,13,14,15,16,17,18
410 DATA  19,20,21,22,23,24,13,0,25,26,27,28,32,31,30,29,25
415 DATA  0,33,34,35,36,40,39,38,37,33
417 DATA  0,41,42,43,44,45,41,0,44,46,47,48,0
418 DATA  49,50,51,52,53,54,55,56,57,58,59,60,61,62,63
419 DATA  64,65,66,0,50,67,68,69,70,54,0,69,73,72,56
420 DATA  0,71,55,0,65,74,75,76,77,61,0,76,80,79,59,0,78,60,0
421 DATA  83,84,85,86,87,88,89,90,91,92,93,94,83,82,84,0
422 DATA  85,82,86,0,87,82,88,0,89,82,90,0,91,82,92,0
423 DATA  93,82,94,0,95,96,97,98,99,100,101,102,103,104,105
424 DATA  106,108,110,111,112,95,0,101,104,0,106,107,100
425 DATA  105,0,96,111,0,108,109,97,110,0
426 DATA  77,78,79,0,70,71,72,0
429 R(1)=X(81):R(2)=Y(81):R(3)=Z(81)
430 X(0)=20:Y(0)=-200:Z(0)=15
440 F=0.1:G=1:REM F IS DISTORTION AND G IS MAGNIFICATION
450 S=1:T=IP:REM START AND FINISH POINTS TO ROTATE
470 W=63:U=29:REM W IS WIDTH AND U IS HEIGHT
475 DIM VA(U,W):REM DIMENSION VIDEO ARRAY
480 DIM SA(30,60):REM ARRAY FOR SCREEN DUMP
490 RETURN
500 REM                 BLANK GRAPHICS
510 PRINT CHR$(12);:REM BLANK SCREEN
520 FOR J=-3968 TO -2049
530 POKE J,192
540 NEXT J
550 RETURN
600 REM                 ROTATE POINTS ABOUT AXIS
610 IF B$="X" THEN GOSUB 1700
620 IF B$="Y" THEN GOSUB 1800
630 IF B$="Z" THEN GOSUB 1900
640 RETURN
650 P1=A1-A2:P2=A3-A4
660 L=SQR(P1*P1+P2*P2)
670 IF P2=0 THEN A5=0-(P1<0)*3.141593
```

59

```
680 IF P1=0 THEN A5=SGN(P2)*1.570796
690 IF P2<>0 AND P1<>0 THEN A5=ATN(P2/P1)-(P1<0)*3.141593
700 A5=A5+E:RETURN
800 REM                    TRANSLATE X,Y,Z TO H,U
810 FOR J=1 TO IP
820 DY=Y(J)-Y(0):IF DY<=0 THEN PRINT "DECREASE Y(0)":STOP
830 DX=X(J)-X(0)
840 DZ=Z(J)-Z(0)
850 U(J)=ATN(F*DZ/DY):REM VERTICAL SCREEN POSITION
860 H(J)=ATN(F*DX/DY):REM HORIZONTAL SCREEN POSITION
870 NEXT J
880 MINU=U(1):MAXU=U(1)
890 MINH=H(1):MAXH=H(1)
900 FOR J=1 TO IP
910 IF U(J)<MINU THEN MINU=U(J)
920 IF U(J)>MAXU THEN MAXU=U(J)
930 IF H(J)<MINH THEN MINH=H(J)
940 IF H(J)>MAXH THEN MAXH=H(J)
950 NEXT J
960 DH=MAXH-MINH
970 DU=MAXU-MINU
980 FOR J=1 TO IP
990 H(J)=G*(H(J)-MINH)/DH*W
1000 U(J)=G*(U(J)-MINU)/DU*U
1110 NEXT J
1120 RETURN
1200 REM                DRAW LINES CONNECTING POINTS
1210 FOR J=1 TO IA-1
1220 IF I(J)=0 OR I(J+1)=0 THEN 1340
1230 HH=H(I(J+1))-H(I(J))
1240 UU=U(I(J+1))-U(I(J))
1250 SN=SGN(HH)
1260 IF SN=0 THEN 1360
1270 M=UU/HH
1280 B=U(I(J))-M*H(I(J))
1290 SP=SQR(UU*UU+HH*HH)
1300 FOR K=H(I(J)) TO H(I(J+1)) STEP 0.3*HH/SP
1310 P=M*K+B
1320 GOSUB 1500
1330 NEXT K
1340 NEXT J
1350 RETURN
1360 REM                SLOPE EQUALS INFINITY
1370 K=H(I(J))
1380 IF SGN(UU)=0 THEN P=H(I(J)):GOSUB 1500:GOTO 1340
1390 FOR P=U(I(J)) TO U(I(J+1)) STEP SGN(UU)/5
```

```
1400 GOSUB 1500
1410 NEXT P
1420 GOTO 1340
1500 REM                PLOTTING SUBOUTINE
1510 IF P>U OR P<0 OR K>W OR K<0 THEN RETURN
1520 Q=INT(K)-2112-64*INT(P)
1530 IF Q>-2049 OR Q<-3968 THEN PRINT "OFFSCREEN":STOP
1540 C1=192+2^(2*(2-INT(3*(P-INT(P))))+INT(2*(K-INT(K))))
1550 POKE Q,(PEEK(Q) OR C1)
1555 IF J<25 OR J>40 THEN VA(P,K)=(PEEK(Q) OR C1)
1560 RETURN
1600 REM ROTATION,TRANSLATE,BLANK SCREEN GRAPHICS,DRAW LINES
1610 GOSUB 600:GOSUB 800:IF ID=0 THEN GOSUB 500
1620 IF ID=0 THEN GOSUB 1200:GOSUB 5000
1630 RETURN
1700 REM                X-AXIS ROTATION
1710 FOR J=S TO T
1720 A1=Y(J):A2=R(2):A3=Z(J):A4=R(3)
1730 GOSUB 650
1740 Y(J)=L*COS(A5)+R(2):Z(J)=L*SIN(A5)+R(3)
1750 NEXT J:RETURN
1800 REM                Y-AXIS ROTATION
1810 FOR J=S TO T
1820 A1=X(J):A2=R(1):A3=Z(J):A4=R(3)
1830 GOSUB 650
1840 X(J)=L*COS(A5)+R(1):Z(J)=L*SIN(A5)+R(3)
1850 NEXT J:RETURN
1900 REM                Z-AXIS ROTATION
1910 FOR J=S TO T
1920 A1=X(J):A2=R(1):A3=Y(J):A4=R(2)
1930 GOSUB 650
1940 X(J)=L*COS(A5)+R(1):Y(J)=L*SIN(A5)+R(2)
1950 NEXT J:RETURN
2000 REM                INSTRUCTIONS
2010 PRINT CHR$(12);:REM CLEAR SCREEN (SOME CAN USE CLS).
2020 PRINT:PRINT
2030 PRINT "COMMAND","DESCRIPTION",,"EXAMPLE"
2040 PRINT "---------","-------------",,"-------"
2045 PRINT
2050 PRINT "A NN","ROLL THE SPACECRAFT","A 1.2"
2060 PRINT "B NN","YAW THE SPACECRAFT","B -1.0"
2070 PRINT "C NN","PITCH THE SPACECRAFT","C 0.22"
2075 PRINT
2080 PRINT "D NN","MOVE CRAFT FORWARD OR BACK","D 23"
2090 PRINT "E NN","MOVE SPACECRAFT SIDEWAYS","E -12"
2100 PRINT "F NN","MOVE.CRAFT UP OR DOWN","F 19"
```

```
2105 PRINT
2110 PRINT "G NN","MOVE PORT CARGO BAY DOOR","G 1.3"
2120 PRINT "H NN","MOVE STARBOARD BAY DOOR","H 0.2"
2125 PRINT:PRINT
2130 PRINT:PRINT "ALL MOTIONS ARE FROM YOUR POINT OF VIEW."
2140 RETURN
3000 REM              DEFINE BLOCK GRAPHICS
3010 FOR J=-512 TO -1:POKE J,0:NEXT J
3020 FOR J=1 TO 63:N=J*8-512
3030 FOR I=1 TO 6:M=2^(I-1):IF (J AND M)=0 THEN 3080
3040 N1=N-(I>2)*3-(I>4)*2
3050 N2=N+2-(I>2)*2-(I>4)*3
3060 N3=240+(INT(I/2)=I/2)*225
3070 FOR P=N1 TO N2:POKE P,(PEEK(P) OR N3):NEXT P
3080 NEXT I,J
3090 RETURN
4000 REM              INTERPRET COMMANDS
4005 S=1:T=IP
4010 IF M1$="A" THEN B$="Y":GOSUB 1600:GOTO 4090
4020 IF M1$="B" THEN B$="Z":GOSUB 1600:GOTO 4090
4030 IF M1$="C" THEN B$="X":GOSUB 1600:GOTO 4090
4040 IF M1$="D" THEN GOSUB 5100:GOTO 4090
4050 IF M1$="E" THEN GOSUB 5200:GOTO 4090
4060 IF M1$="F" THEN GOSUB 5300:GOTO 4090
4070 IF M1$="G" THEN GOSUB 5500:GOTO 4090
4080 IF M1$="H" THEN GOSUB 5400
4090 RETURN
5000 REM    RECORD MANIPULATIONS
5010 PTR=PTR+1:SN(PTR)=E:STL(PTR)=ASC(M1$)
5020 RETURN
5100 REM    MOVE IN THE X DIRECTION
5110 FOR J=S TO T:X(J)=X(J)+E:NEXT J
5120 GOSUB 5000:RETURN
5200 REM    MOVE IN THE Y DIRECTION
5210 FOR J=S TO T:Y(J)=Y(J)+E:NEXT J
5220 GOSUB 5000:RETURN
5300 REM    MOVE IN THE Z DIRECTION
5310 FOR J=S TO T:Z(J)=Z(J)+E:NEXT J
5320 GOSUB 5000:RETURN
5400 REM    MOVE CARGO BAY DOORS
5410 S=33:T=40:B$="X":R(1)=SX(36):R(2)=SY(36)
5415 R(3)=SZ(36):REM FOR STARBOARD BAY DOORS
5420 FOR J=S TO T:X(J)=SX(J):Y(J)=SY(J):Z(J)=SZ(J)
5425 NEXT J:GOSUB 600:R(1)=X(81):R(2)=Y(81):R(3)=Z(81)
5430 ID=1:FOR K=1 TO PTR
5440 M1$=CHR$(STL(K)):E=SN(K)
```

```
5450 GOSUB 4010:NEXT KK:ID=0
5460 GOSUB 800:GOSUB 500:GOSUB 1200:RETURN
5510 S=25:T=32:B$="X":R(1)=SX(28):R(2)=SY(28)
5520 R(3)=SZ(28):GOSUB 5420:RETURN
5520 GOSUB 5420:RETURN
6000 REM    OPTIONAL SCREEN DUMP TO PRINTER
6010 FOR J=1 TO 30:FOR K=1 TO 60
6020 SA(J,K)=PEEK(64*(J-1)+K-3969):NEXT K,J
6030 N1=3*2^INT(6*RND(1))
6040 POKE 260,0:POKE 261,0:POKE 0,62:POKE 1,27
6050 POKE 2,205:POKE 3,12:POKE 4,224:POKE 5,201
6060 XX=USR(0):POKE 1,65:XX=USR(0):POKE 1,2:XX=USR(0)
6070 FOR J=1 TO 30:FOR L=-8 TO -1
6080 FOR K=0 TO 59:IF K/15=INT(K/15) THEN GOSUB 6120
6090 CN=PEEK(L-8*(255-SA(J,K+1))):FOR M=7 TO 0 STEP -1
6100 POKE 1,N1*SGN(CN AND 2^M):XX=USR(0):NEXT M,K
6110 POKE 1,13:XX=USR(0):NEXT L,J:POKE 1,12:XX=USR(0):RETURN
6120 POKE 1,27:XX=USR(0):POKE 1,75:XX=USR(0)
6130 POKE 1,120:XX=USR(0):POKE 1,0:XX=USR(0):RETURN
READY
```

We now look at the lines of the program. Lines 10-35 give the remarks about the program. Line 40 clears the video screen. Line 41 prints three blank lines and lines 42-44 print out the name of the program on the screen. Line 45 prints three more blank lines, and then line 46 asks whether or not you want to see the instructions for the program. If the answer is yes, line 47 sends program control to the subroutine at line 2000. After three more print statements in line 48, the computer tells us that it is setting up the program (line 49). Line 50 is a subroutine call to line 3000, which defines the block-type graphics. Delete this line if your computer uses the set or reset commands, if it cannot define graphic characters, or if it doesn't conform for any reason. Line 60 is a subroutine call to line 300, which reads the coordinates of the data points and the lines that connect them, dimensions the arrays, and sets variables. Line 65 contains the subroutine calls that display the first figure. Line 70 requests you to enter the command to manipulate the computer model. Line 75 breaks the reply up into the alphabetic and numerical portions and assigns them to M1$ and E, respectively. Line 80 is a subroutine call to line 4000, which interprets the commands.

Line 90 is an optional line, which should be used only when you want a hard copy of the figures on the screen. It is a call to a subroutine that sends the image to the printer. Line 100 goes to line 70, where the next command is requested.

Lines 300-490 contain the statements that initialize the program. Line 300 is the remark statement for the heading. Line 305 says that IP, the number of points, is 112 and IA, the number of line connections, is 187. PTR is the index of a stack that we are going to use when operating the cargo bay doors. ID is a variable that indicates the level of subroutine calls, also for the cargo bay door operation. Line 310 dimensions the line connection array, I, the X, Y, and Z-coordinate arrays, and R, V, and H. Line 315 dimensions an array for a stack of command letters, and line 316 dimensions the arrays that contain the coordinates of the points at the start of the program, for use with the door manipulations. Line 318 contains the array for the stack of numbers also used for the doors. The loop in lines 320-340 reads in the data for the coordinates at the start of the program.

Lines 345-371 contain data statements for the X, Y, and Z coordinate of each point. Lines 380-400

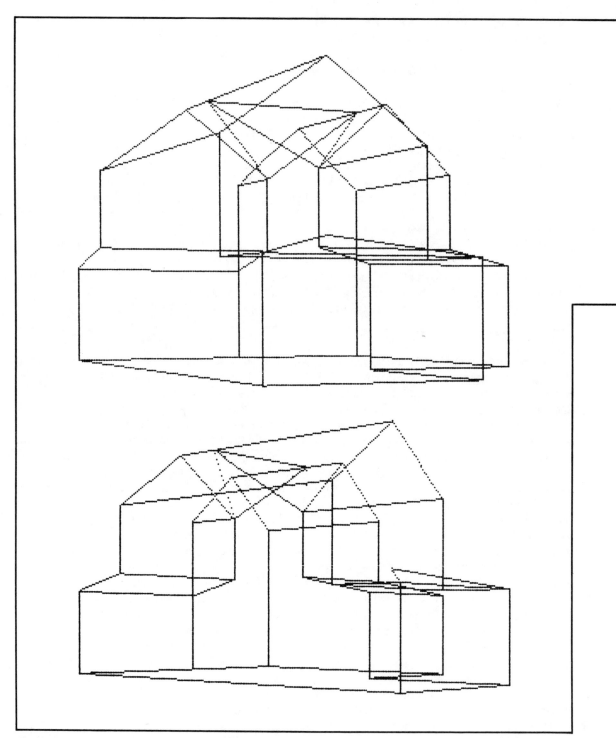

Fig. 4-2. Perspective line drawing of house (three views).

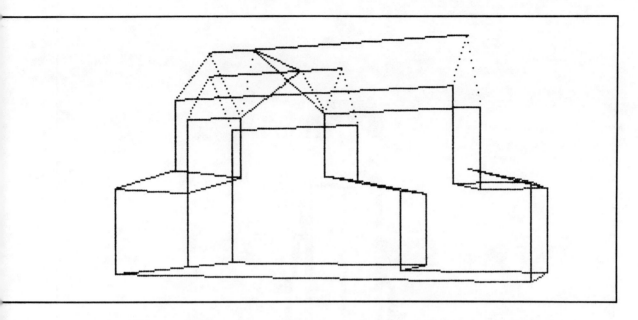

read in the connection array from the data statements in lines 405-426. Line 429 sets the points about which the craft will rotate. For all three axis the coordinate of the point is 81. Line 430 sets the viewpoint's coordinates, and line 440 sets F and G. Line 450 sets the values of S and T, the first and the last points that we want to rotate. Line 470 sets the width and height of the video screen, minus 1. You may change this for your computer. If your computer uses set and reset, you may want to use 127 and 47. Line 480 dimensions an array for a screen dump. Line 490 returns control back to line 65.

The subroutine in lines 500-550 blanks the screen dump. Line 490 returns control back to line 65.

The subroutine in lines 500-550 blanks the screen. Another method of blanking the screen is to use a loop that resets J and K. Where J is the loop from 0 to U and K is a nested loop from 0 to W. Other computers may require a different technique.

The subroutine in lines 600-700, which uses subroutines at lines 1700, 1800, and 1900, rotates points about an axis in exactly the same way as the rotation subroutines that we saw earlier did. However, this subroutine is faster. Lines 800-1120 form a subroutine that translates the points into vertical and horizontal positions for use on the screen. It is

the same as ones that we've seen before. Lines 1200-1420 contain the familiar subroutine that draws lines connecting points. Lines 1500-1560 are a plotting subroutine that is rather system-specific. If your computer uses set, you might change lines 1520-1555 to SET(K,P). This command turns on a screen element on some systems.

Lines 1700-1750 are part of the rotation subroutine that rotates points around the X-axis. Lines 1800-1850 are part of the subroutine that rotates points around the Y-axis, and lines 1900-1950 rotate points about the Z-axis. Lines 2000-2140 form the subroutine that prints the instructions. The first six commands move the spacecraft using our reference system. If we type A 1.5, the model turns about 90 degrees counterclockwise on the screen. Lines 3000-3090 form a subroutine that defines user-defined graphic characters. It may not work on your system, or you may not need them as we stated earlier. I won't explain how these statements are defined, except to say that they create graphic characters that are a 3×2 rectangular block of squares.

The commands for the program are interpreted by the subroutine in lines 4000-5520. Lines 4010-4080 transfer control to appropriate subroutine for the letter entered. Lines 5000-5020

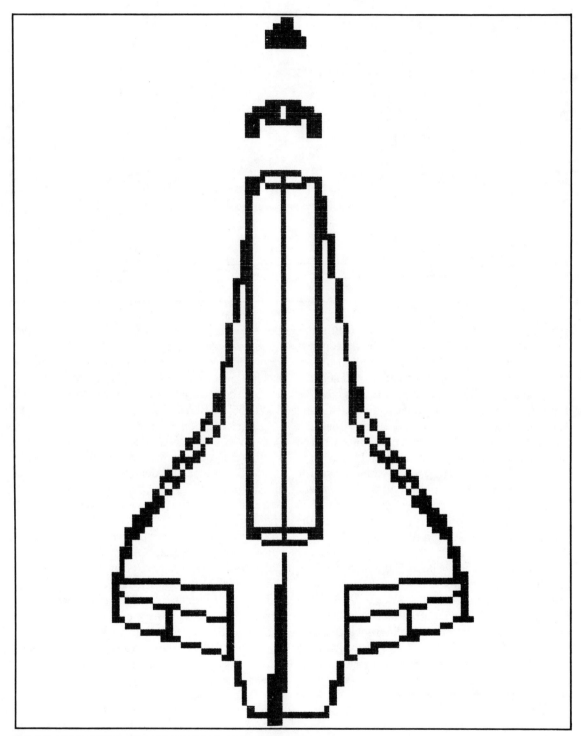

Fig. 4-3. Low-resolution video display of a space shuttle model.

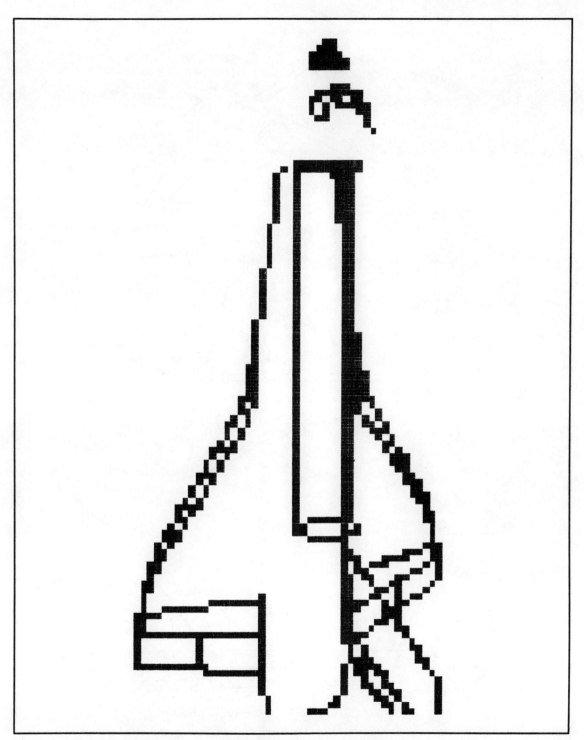

Fig. 4-4. Low-resolution video display of a space shuttle model as it is rotated.

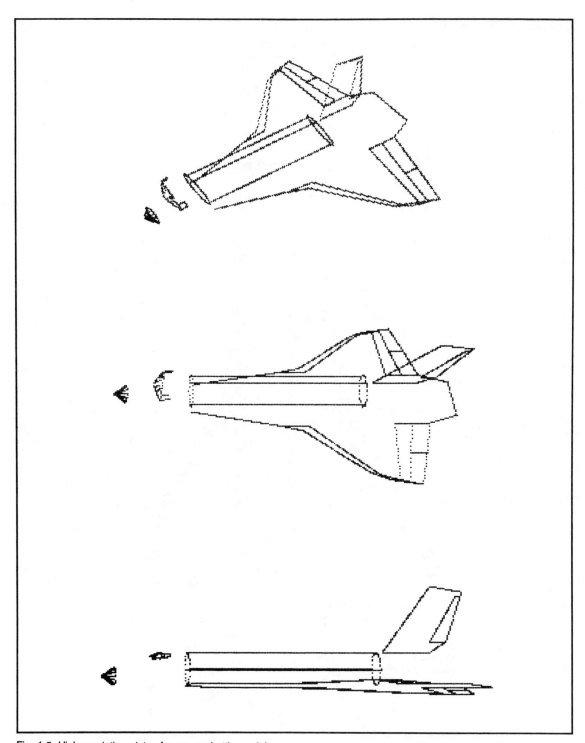

Fig. 4-5. High-resolution plots of a space shuttle model.

record the commands if they are the motion of the entire craft, i.e., letters A-F. Lines 5100-5120 are for motion in the X-direction; 5200-5220 are for motion in the Y-direction; 5300-5320 are for motion in the Z-direction. The number entered is simply added to each points' coordinates in whatever dimension it is moved.

Lines 5400-5520 are statements for the operation of the cargo bay doors. A positive number will cause the doors to open and a negative number will cause them to close. These numbers should not have values outside of the range of −1.6 to 1.6 or the doors will appear to pass through the wings. We should also note that you should not use large numbers when moving the spacecraft as the points could shift off the screen, out of the field of vision and you would be lost.

When a command is received to operate the starboard bay door, the program will run through lines 5400-5460. With the port door, lines 5500-5520 are called. They in turn also call lines 5420-5460 of the starboard call. This is simply a space-saving technique since the routine is the same; only the points involved and the p oints of rotation are different. In line 5410 S is set to 33 and T is set to 40. These are the first and last points of the starboard bay door. Rotation is about the X-axis since that is the axis they rotate about at the start of the program. Point 36 is the point of one of the hinges of the door and we use that point for the axis of rota-

tion. On the starboard door, we set E equal to negative E since a positive number opens the door. Line 5420 defines the points of the door as their original values at the start. Line 5425 performs the opening rotation on the door and sets the point of rotation back to the original 81. Lines 5430-5460 is a stack reading loop that manipulates the points through all the commands that the computer has received up to this point. This is the method of putting the doors back on the model.

What we actually accomplish with this subroutine is to rotate the cargo bay doors about an arbitrary axis. We rotated the doors about their original axis, the X-axis, then went through the stack of all the manipulations to move the points of the doors back to where they should now be relative to the rest of the model.

Lines 6000-6130 are the subroutine for the optional screen dump to printer. We will not discuss it here as we have already covered it in other programs.

A High-Resolution Perspective Line Program—Program 11

This program is the same, in many respects, as the low-resolution version. However, the images created by this version are meant to be printed on paper. No pictures appear on the video display. The program draws a much finer line when printing the pictures.

```
10 REM       HIGH-RESOLUTION SPACE SHUTTLE SIMULATION
20 REM          WRITTEN BY TIMOTHY J. O'MALLEY
30 REM           COPYRIGHT 1982, TAB BOOKS INC.
35 REM
40 PRINT CHR$(12);
41 PRINT:PRINT:PRINT
42 PRINT TAB(15);"INTERACTIVE SPACE SHUTTLE SIMULATION"
43 PRINT TAB(18);"WRITTEN BY TIMOTHY J. O'MALLEY"
44 PRINT TAB(18);"COPYRIGHT 1982, TAB BOOKS INC."
45 PRINT:PRINT:PRINT
46 INPUT "DO YOU WANT INSTRUCTIONS (YES OR NO)";AN$
47 IF AN$="YES" THEN GOSUB 2000
48 PRINT:PRINT:PRINT
49 PRINT "THE COMPUTER WILL NOW SET UP THE PROGRAM."
60 GOSUB 300:REM    INITIALIZE VARIABLES
```

```
65  GOSUB 500:GOSUB 800:GOSUB 1200:GOSUB 6000:REM DISPLAY START
70  INPUT "COMMAND";CM$
75  M1$=LEFT$(CM$,1):E=VAL(RIGHT$(CM$,(LEN(CM$)-2)))
80  GOSUB 4000:REM    INTERPRET COMMANDS
90  GOSUB 6000:REM PRINT OUT IN HIGH RESOLUTION
100 GOTO 70
300 REM                  INITIALIZE VARIABLES
305 IP=112:IA=187:PTR=0:ID=0
310 DIM I(IA),X(IP),Y(IP),Z(IP),R(3),V(IP),H(IP)
315 DIM STL(50)
316 DIM SX(IP),SY(IP),SZ(IP)
318 DIM SN(50)
320 FOR J=1 TO IP
330 READ X(J),Y(J),Z(J)
335 SX(J)=X(J):SY(J)=Y(J):SZ(J)=Z(J)
340 NEXT J
345 DATA 0,0,0, 0,3.75,1, 0,6.5,3.75, 0,7.5,7.5
346 DATA 0,6.5,11.25, 0,3.5,14, 0,0,15, 0,-3.75,14
347 DATA 0,-6.5,11.25, 0,-7.5,7.5, 0,-6.5,3.75,0,-3.75,1
348 DATA 60,0,0, 60,3.75,1,60,6.5,3.75,60,7.5,7.5
349 DATA 60,6.5,11.25,60,3.75,14,60,0,15,60,-3.75,14
350 DATA 60,-6.5,11.25,60,-7.5,7.5,60,-6.5,3.75,60,-3.75,1
351 DATA 0,0,15,0,-3.75,14,0,-6.5,11.25,0,-7.5,7.5
352 DATA 60,0,15,60,-3.75,14,60,-6.5,11.25,60,-7.5,7.5
353 DATA 0,0,15,0,3.75,14,0,6.5,11.25,0,7.5,7.5
354 DATA 60,0,15,60,3.75,14,60,6.5,11.25,60,7.5,7.5
355 DATA 62,0,15,77,0,45,87,0,42.5,82,0,20
356 DATA 77,0,15,77,0,20,85,0,40.5,86,0,40.5
357 DATA 0,-7.5,0,31,-14.5,0,39,-17,0,60,-37,0,66,-40,0
358 DATA 76,-42,0,79.5,-28,0,83,-13,0,93,-9,0,93,9,0
359 DATA 83,13,0,79.5,28,0,76,42,0,66,40,0,60,37,0
360 DATA 39,17,0,31,14.5,0,0,7.5,0,41.5,-15,0,63,-38,0
361 DATA 69,-40,0,72,-41,0,74,-28,0,77,-13,0,71,-13,0
362 DATA 41.5,15,0,63,38,0,69,40,0,72,41,0,74,28,0
363 DATA 77,13,0, 71,13,0, 30,7.5,7.5
364 DATA -28,0,4,-24,0,8,-24,-2,7.5,-24,-3.5,6,-24,-4,4
365 DATA -24,-3.5,2,-24,-2,.5,-24,0,0,-24,2,.5,-24,3.5,2
366 DATA -24,4,4,-24,3.5,6,-24,2,7.5,-6.5,-6,14.5
367 DATA -9,-6,14.5,-10,-3,14.5,-9,-3,15,-9,3,15
368 DATA -10,3,14.5,-9,6,14.5,-6.5,6,14.5,-6.5,7.5,13
369 DATA -10,7.5,12,-11.5,3.5,13,-12.5,1,13,-10,1.5,14.5
370 DATA -12.5,-1,13,-10,-1.5,14.5,-11.5,-3.5,13
371 DATA -10,-7.5,12,-6.5,-7.5,13
380 FOR J=1 TO IA
390 READ I(J)
400 NEXT J
```

```
405 DATA 1,2,3,4,5,6,7,8,9,10,11,12,1,0,13,14,15,16,17,18
410 DATA 19,20,21,22,23,24,13,0,25,26,27,28,32,31,30,29,25
415 DATA 0,33,34,35,36,40,39,38,37,33
417 DATA 0,41,42,43,44,45,41,0,44,46,47,48,0
418 DATA 49,50,51,52,53,54,55,56,57,58,59,60,61,62,63
419 DATA 64,65,66,0,50,67,68,69,70,54,0,69,73,72,56
420 DATA 0,71,55,0,65,74,75,76,77,61,0,76,80,79,59,0,78,60,0
421 DATA 83,84,85,86,87,88,89,90,91,92,93,94,83,82,84,0
422 DATA 85,82,86,0,87,82,88,0,89,82,90,0,91,82,92,0
423 DATA 93,82,94,0,95,96,97,98,99,100,101,102,103,104,105
424 DATA 106,108,110,111,112,95,0,101,104,0,106,107,100
425 DATA 105,0,96,111,0,108,109,97,110,0
426 DATA 77,78,79,0,70,71,72,0
429 R(1)=X(81):R(2)=Y(81):R(3)=Z(81)
430 X(0)=20:Y(0)=-200:Z(0)=15
440 F=0.1:G=1:REM F IS DISTORTION AND G IS MAGNIFICATION
450 S=1:T=IP:REM START AND FINISH POINTS TO ROTATE
470 W=253:U=17:W2=127
475 DIM VA(U,W):REM DIMENSION VIDEO ARRAY
490 RETURN
500 REM           BLANK ARRAY
510 PRINT CHR$(12);:REM BLANK SCREEN
520 FOR JS=0 TO U:FOR KS=0 TO W
530 VA(JS,KS)=0
540 NEXT KS,JS
550 RETURN
600 REM                 ROTATE POINTS ABOUT AXIS
610 IF B$="X" THEN GOSUB 1700
620 IF B$="Y" THEN GOSUB 1800
630 IF B$="Z" THEN GOSUB 1900
640 RETURN
650 P1=A1-A2:P2=A3-A4
660 L=SQR(P1*P1+P2*P2)
670 IF P2=0 THEN A5=0-(P1<0)*3.141593
680 IF P1=0 THEN A5=SGN(P2)*1.570796
690 IF P2<>0 AND P1<>0 THEN A5=ATN(P2/P1)-(P1<0)*3.141593
700 A5=A5+E:RETURN
800 REM                 TRANSLATE X,Y,Z TO H,V
810 FOR J=1 TO IP
820 DY=Y(J)-Y(0):IF DY<=0 THEN PRINT "DECREASE Y(0)":STOP
830 DX=X(J)-X(0)
840 DZ=Z(J)-Z(0)
850 V(J)=ATN(F*DZ/DY):REM VERTICAL SCREEN POSITION
860 H(J)=ATN(F*DX/DY):REM HORIZONTAL SCREEN POSITION
870 NEXT J
880 MINV=V(1):MAXV=V(1)
```

```
890 MINH=H(1):MAXH=H(1)
900 FOR J=1 TO IP
910 IF V(J)<MINV THEN MINV=V(J)
920 IF V(J)>MAXV THEN MAXV=V(J)
930 IF H(J)<MINH THEN MINH=H(J)
940 IF H(J)>MAXH THEN MAXH=H(J)
950 NEXT J
960 DH=MAXH-MINH
970 DV=MAXV-MINV
980 FOR J=1 TO IP
990 H(J)=G*(H(J)-MINH)/DH*W
1000 V(J)=G*(V(J)-MINV)/DV*U
1110 NEXT J
1120 RETURN
1200 REM               DRAW LINES CONNECTING POINTS
1210 FOR J=1 TO IA-1
1220 IF I(J)=0 OR I(J+1)=0 THEN 1340
1230 HH=H(I(J+1))-H(I(J))
1240 VV=V(I(J+1))-V(I(J))
1250 SN=SGN(HH)
1260 IF SN=0 THEN 1360
1270 M=VV/HH
1280 B=V(I(J))-M*H(I(J))
1290 SP=SQR(VV*VV+HH*HH)
1300 FOR K=H(I(J)) TO H(I(J+1)) STEP 0.3*HH/SP
1310 P=M*K+B
1320 GOSUB 1500
1330 NEXT K
1340 NEXT J
1350 RETURN
1360 REM               SLOPE EQUALS INFINITY
1370 K=H(I(J))
1380 IF SGN(VV)=0 THEN P=H(I(J)):GOSUB 1500:GOTO 1340
1390 FOR P=V(I(J)) TO V(I(J+1)) STEP SGN(VV)/12
1400 GOSUB 1500
1410 NEXT P
1420 GOTO 1340
1500 REM               PLOTTING SUBOUTINE
1510 IF P>U OR P<0 OR K>W OR K<0 THEN RETURN
1520 V1=INT(P):V2=INT(K)
1530 VA(V1,V2)=VA(V1,V2) OR 2^INT(12*(P-V1))
1560 RETURN
1600 REM ROTATION,TRANSLATE,BLANK SCREEN GRAPHICS,DRAW
     LINES
1610 GOSUB 600:GOSUB 800:IF ID=0 THEN GOSUB 500
1620 IF ID=0 THEN GOSUB 1200:GOSUB 5000
```

```
1630 RETURN
1700 REM              X-AXIS ROTATION
1710 FOR J=S TO T
1720 A1=Y(J):A2=R(2):A3=Z(J):A4=R(3)
1730 GOSUB 650
1740 Y(J)=L*COS(A5)+R(2):Z(J)=L*SIN(A5)+R(3)
1750 NEXT J:RETURN
1800 REM              Y-AXIS ROTATION
1810 FOR J=S TO T
1820 A1=X(J):A2=R(1):A3=Z(J):A4=R(3)
1830 GOSUB 650
1840 X(J)=L*COS(A5)+R(1):Z(J)=L*SIN(A5)+R(3)
1850 NEXT J:RETURN
1900 REM              Z-AXIS ROTATION
1910 FOR J=S TO T
1920 A1=X(J):A2=R(1):A3=Y(J):A4=R(2)
1930 GOSUB 650
1940 X(J)=L*COS(A5)+R(1):Y(J)=L*SIN(A5)+R(2)
1950 NEXT J:RETURN
2000 REM              INSTRUCTIONS
2020 PRINT:PRINT
2030 PRINT "COMMAND","DESCRIPTION",,"EXAMPLE"
2040 PRINT "-------","------------",,"-------"
2045 PRINT
2050 PRINT "A NN","ROLL THE SPACECRAFT","A 1.2"
2060 PRINT "B NN","YAW THE SPACECRAFT","B -1.0"
2070 PRINT "C NN","PITCH THE SPACECRAFT","C 0.22"
2075 PRINT
2080 PRINT "D NN","MOVE CRAFT FORWARD OR BACK","D 23"
2090 PRINT "E NN","MOVE SPACECRAFT SIDEWAYS","E -12"
2100 PRINT "F NN","MOVE CRAFT UP OR DOWN","F 19"
2105 PRINT
2110 PRINT "G NN","MOVE PORT CARGO BAY DOOR","G 1.3"
2120 PRINT "H NN","MOVE STARBOARD BAY DOOR","H 0.2"
2125 PRINT:PRINT
2130 PRINT:PRINT "ALL MOTIONS ARE FROM YOUR POINT OF VIEW."
2140 RETURN
4000 REM              INTERPRET COMMANDS
4005 S=1:T=IP
4010 IF M1$="A" THEN B$="Y":GOSUB 1600:GOTO 4090
4020 IF M1$="B" THEN B$="Z":GOSUB 1600:GOTO 4090
4030 IF M1$="C" THEN B$="X":GOSUB 1600:GOTO 4090
4040 IF M1$="D" THEN GOSUB 5100:GOTO 4090
4050 IF M1$="E" THEN GOSUB 5200:GOTO 4090
4060 IF M1$="F" THEN GOSUB 5300:GOTO 4090
4070 IF M1$="G" THEN GOSUB 5500:GOTO 4090
```

```
4080 IF M1$="H" THEN GOSUB 5400
4090 RETURN
5000 REM     RECORD MANIPULATIONS
5010 PTR=PTR+1:SN(PTR)=E:STL(PTR)=ASC(M1$)
5020 RETURN
5100 REM     MOVE IN THE X DIRECTION
5110 FOR J=S TO T:X(J)=X(J)+E:NEXT J
5120 GOSUB 5000:RETURN
5200 REM     MOVE IN THE Y DIRECTION
5210 FOR J=S TO T:Y(J)=Y(J)+E:NEXT J
5220 GOSUB 5000:RETURN
5300 REM     MOVE IN THE Z DIRECTION
5310 FOR J=S TO T:Z(J)=Z(J)+E:NEXT J
5320 GOSUB 5000:RETURN
5400 REM     MOVE CARGO BAY DOORS
5410 S=33:T=40:B$="X":R(1)=SX(36):R(2)=SY(36)
5415 R(3)=SZ(36):REM FOR STARBOARD BAY DOORS
5420 FOR J=S TO T:X(J)=SX(J):Y(J)=SY(J):Z(J)=SZ(J)
5425 NEXT J:GOSUB 600:R(1)=X(81):R(2)=Y(81):R(3)=Z(81)
5430 ID=1:FOR KK=1 TO PTR
5440 M1$=CHR$(STL(KK)):E=SN(KK)
5450 GOSUB 4010:NEXT KK:ID=0
5460 GOSUB 800:GOSUB 500:GOSUB 1200:RETURN
5500 REM     MOVE PORT CARGO BAY DOOR
5510 S=25:T=32:B$="X":R(1)=SX(28):R(2)=SY(28)
5520 R(3)=SZ(28):GOSUB 5420:RETURN
6000 REM          HIGH-RESOLUTION PRINTER
6005 GOSUB 7000:REM SET UP SUBROUTINE FOR PRINTER
6010 FOR JS=U TO 0 STEP -1:FOR MS=11 TO 0 STEP -1
6020 BS=INT(2^MS):FOR LS=0 TO 1:GOSUB 6050
6030 FOR KS=LS*W2 TO LS*W2+W2-1:POKE 1,SGN(BS AND VA(JS,KS))
6040 XX=USR(0):NEXT KS,LS:POKE 1,13:XX=USR(0):NEXT MS,JS
6045 RETURN
6050 POKE 1,27:XX=USR(0):POKE 1,75:XX=USR(0):POKE 1,W2
6060 XX=USR(0):POKE 1,0:XX=USR(0):RETURN
7000 REM          SET UP MACHINE LANGUAGE SUBROUTINE FOR PRINTER
7010 POKE 260,0:POKE 261,0:POKE 0,62:POKE 1,27:POKE 2,205
7020 POKE 3,12:POKE 4,224:POKE 5,201:XX=USR(0):POKE 1,65
7030 XX=USR(0):POKE 1,1:XX=USR(0):RETURN
READY
```

Let's look at the lines that are different. Line 10 indicates that this is a high-resolution program. We have deleted line 50, lines 3000-3090, and lines 6070-6130, along with lines 2010, 1540-1555, and line 480. Lines 1520 and 1530 have been changed because we are using a different plotting subroutine. This plotting subroutine is the same type as the one that we used when we drew the perspective line drawing of the house. Line 470 was changed to make W=253, U=18 and W2=127. We

```
       INTERACTIVE SPACE SHUTTLE SIMULATION
          WRITTEN BY TIMOTHY J. O'MALLEY
          COPYRIGHT 1982, TAB BOOKS INC.


  DO YOU WANT INSTRUCTIONS (YES OR NO)? YES


  COMMAND          DESCRIPTION                   EXAMPLE
  --- ---          --- --- --- ---               --- ---


  A NN             ROLL THE SPACECRAFT           A 1.2
  B NN             YAW THE SPACECRAFT            B -1.0
  C NN             PITCH THE SPACECRAFT          C 0.22

  D NN             MOVE CRAFT FORWARD OR BACK    D 23
  E NN             MOVE SPACECRAFT SIDEWAYS      E -12
  F NN             MOVE CRAFT UP OR DOWN         F 19

  G NN             MOVE PORT CARGO BAY DOOR      G 1.3
  H NN             MOVE STARBOARD BAY DOOR       H 0.2



  ALL MOTIONS ARE FROM YOUR POINT OF VIEW.



  THE COMPUTER WILL NOW SET UP THE PROGRAM.
```

Fig. 4-6. Display of instructions for space shuttle simulation.

added a subroutine at lines 7000-7030 to set up the machine-language routine for the high-resolution printer. We changed the subroutine at lines 500-550, which blanked the graphics. Now it sets all the elements in the VA array to zero. We changed the printer subroutine, which starts at line 6000.

Figure 4-5 shows how the model appears after some manipulations. Fig. 4-6 shows what the video display looks like if you request instructions. Both programs are essentially the same in their operation. We will discuss high-resolution a little more in the next chapter, along with line elimination.

Chapter 5

High-Resolution Graphics and Line Elimination

This chapter discusses high-resolution graphics and the hidden line problem, and contains four BASIC programs which create large-scale high-resolution plotters and three-dimensional solid figure plotters.

DEFINING HIGH- AND LOW-RESOLUTION GRAPHICS

Let's define some terms concerning resolution in graphics. We will consider low-resolution figures to the figures drawn using alphanumeric characters as symbols. In the first histogram program we used the uppercase letter H as a graphic symbol. The images created using the lowercase letter o, the plus sign, and other similar symbols to create images are examples of low-resolution graphics. High-resolution shall be defined as the use of symbols where more than one position of a point can lie within the area occupied by a low-resolution symbol. Our low-resolution space shuttle model was really a high-resolution figure since we used tiny squares to represent the points and about four of those squares equaled the area oc-cupied by an alphanumeric character. We called it low-resolution to distinguish it from the second shuttle program, which had greater resolution.

Types of Graphic Characters

Some computers have a predefined graphic character set for creating high-resolution graphic images. Some use a block-type of graphic set and the characters have ASCII codes above 127. To print the graphic character, you would simply de-termine the code number of the character that you want to print and enter **PRINT CHR$(X)**, where X is the code number. By placing this character at the proper position, you can create a graphic image. Other computers use much the same technique except the characters used can be straight lines in all directions, curved lines, or special figures like those used in Fig. 1-1.

Other computers allow you to define your own graphic characters. You or your computer can make a user-defined graphic set, which can be very use-ful. The images in Fig. 5-1 were made using a

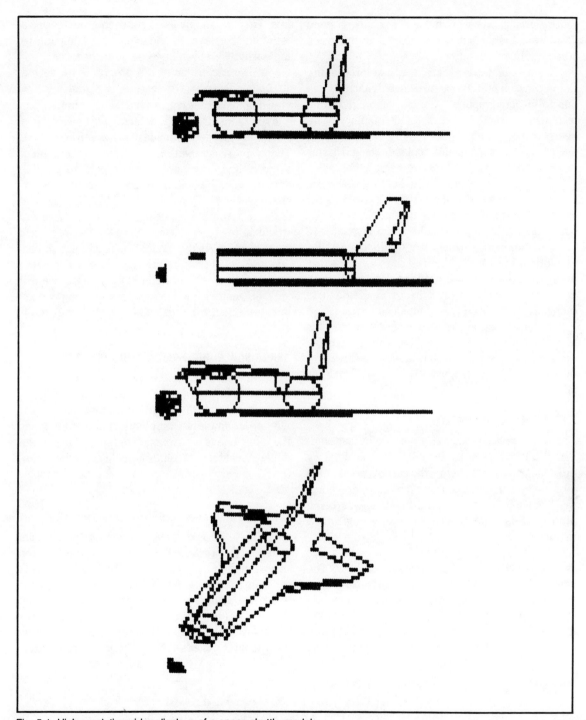

Fig. 5-1. High-resolution video displays of a space shuttle model.

shuttle simulation program that defined the graphic characters and displayed the images on the video screen in high-resolution.

Some computers skip the use of graphic characters completely and turn on individual screen bits to display graphics. The disadvantage of this technique is that it uses a lot of memory. The microcomputer industry is rapidly changing, and even as you are reading this book, bigger and better ways of displaying graphics are being invented.

Dot matrix printers create their alphanumeric characters using a 7×5 dot matrix. Many computers also show alphanumerics on the video screen using this method. If we could coax a computer to print out individual dots, we would have high-resolution. In fact, the high-resolution figures that we made of the house were made by programming a dot matrix printer to print in terms of the dots themselves, not in terms of alphanumerics.

Some computers use an 8×8 dot matrix for displaying characters. Since a lot of microcomputers are 8-bit systems, each character, particularly the graphics characters, would consist of eight 8-bit numbers.

THE HIDDEN LINE PROBLEM

We have seen several ways to eliminate hidden points. In program 3 and 4, it was done by erasing all the points below the current point being plotted. Because we used functions and were working from left to right as the function was being plotted, this type of erasing was a legitimate method to use.

What happens when we want to make a line drawing and delete the lines that do not show? The computer has no way of knowing that certain lines should not be visible. We have seen some algorithms that will eliminate hidden lines. Generally they are number-crunchers which use a lot of time. We really must find another way to represent the

data. We can't simply use a set of coordinates and a list of line connections and expect the computer to know what we consider to be solid surfaces.

In the molecular model program, we sorted the points according to decreasing distance to the viewpoint. We then considered that anything within a given radius from the molecule was a surface of the sphere and points inside of it were to be erased. That was an easy solution but it could not be applied to other line drawings. One approach to the line drawing model would be to designate surfaces instead of lines. The lines could be the edges of surfaces. Another solution, for simple figures, would be to store what lines are visible from each point of view. As the model was manipulated, certain lines would not be printed. That would effectively eliminate them. Later in this chapter we will look at another methods for eliminating hidden lines within three-dimensional solid figure plotters.

LARGE-SCALE, HIGH-RESOLUTION PLOTTERS

We will now look at two programs that are capable of plotting in high-resolution but that covers a larger area than the programs that we saw earlier. One program plots data points and functions, and the other one is an expanded version of the three-dimensional function plotter we discussed in Chapter 3.

A Data Point Plotter in BASIC—Program 12

Figure 5-2 is the result of running the program called *High Resolution Plotter,* using the function that is defined in line 15 of the program. This program can plot either (X, Y) points or a function in which Y is a function of X. In the figure, we labeled the axis and the graph as a whole. The points are individual points so this program will not work on all computers. Let's look at the program listing.

```
3 REM              HIGH RESOLUTION PLOTTER
4 REM              WRITTEN BY TIMOTHY J. O'MALLEY
5 REM              COPYRIGHT 1982, TAB BOOKS INC.
6 REM              ALL RIGHTS RESERVED.
7 REM
```

```
10 CLEAR 100
15 DEF FNA(T)=SIN(LOG(T))
20 DP=100
30 DIM X(DP),Y(DP),Z(DP),W(DP),G(DP),H(DP),M(DP),N(DP)
35 DIM GT(50),AT(50),OT(25)
40 PRINT CHR$(12);
50 PRINT:PRINT:PRINT
60 PRINTTAB(21);"1    1 111   111   1     1"
70 PRINTTAB(21);"1    1 1   1       1     1"
80 PRINTTAB(21);"11111  1   1 111 11111"
90 PRINTTAB(21);"1    1 1   1   1 1     1"
100 PRINTTAB(21);"1    1 111   111   1     1"
110 PRINT:PRINT
115 PRINT TAB(3);
120 PRINT"1111  11111  1111  111  1     1    1 11111 111  111";
130 PRINT"  1    1"
135 PRINT TAB(3);
140 PRINT"1   1 1    1     1    1 1   1   1   1   1    ";
150 PRINT"1 11   1"
155 PRINT TAB(3);
160 PRINT"1111   1111    111   1   1 1   1   1   1   1    ";
170 PRINT"1 1 1 1"
175 PRINT TAB(3);
180 PRINT"1   1  1          1 1   1 1   1   1   1   1    ";
190 PRINT"1 1   11"
195 PRINT TAB(3);
200 PRINT"1    1 11111 1111   111 11111 111   1   111  111";
210 PRINT"  1    1"
220 PRINT:PRINT
230 PRINTTAB(11);"1111  1      111  11111 11111 11111 1111"
240 PRINTTAB(11);"1    1 1     1   1 1     1     1     1    1"
250 PRINTTAB(11);"1111  1     1   1 1     1     1111  1111"
260 PRINTTAB(11);"1     1     1   1 1     1     1     1   1"
270 PRINTTAB(11);"1     11111  111   1     1     11111 1    1"
275 GOSUB 4000
280 PRINT:PRINT:PRINT
285 INPUT "DO YOU WANT INSTRUCTIONS (YES OR NO)";AN$
286 IF AN$="YES" THEN GOSUB 3000
287 GOSUB 2600
290 GOSUB 500:REM        DEFINE GRAPHING PARAMETERS
295 GOSUB 5000:REM SCREEN DUMP TO PRINTER
300 END
400 REM SUBROUTINE (400-480) DEFINES 1ST OR 2ND VARIABLES
410 FOR I=255 TO 0 STEP -5
420 PRINT "ENTER ONE NUMBER PER LINE. WHEN DONE TYPE: END"
430 INPUT Q1$
```

```
440 IF Q1$="END" THEN RETURN
450 K1=K1+1
460 IF J1=1 THEN X(K1)=VAL(Q1$):X(0)=K1
470 IF J1=2 THEN Y(K1)=VAL(Q1$):Y(0)=K1
480 GOTO 430
500 REM SUBROUTINE (500-600) INPUTS GRAPHING PARAMETERS
510 GOSUB 900:PRINT "LIST OF GRAPHING PARAMETERS:"
520 PRINT:FOR J1=1 TO 10:READ A1$:PRINT A1$:NEXT J1
530 RESTORE:PRINT:INPUT "WHICH PARAMETER";Q2$
540 FOR J1=1 TO 10:READ A1$
550 IF A1$<>Q2$ THEN 560
555 ONJ1GOSUB400,400,700,2100,2200,2100,2200,1700,1400,1600
560 IF Q2$="END" THEN END
570 NEXT J1:RESTORE:IF Q2$<>"INITIATE GRAPHING" THEN 500
575 RETURN
580 DATA DEFINE 1ST VARIABLE SET,DEFINE 2ND VARIABLE SET
585 DATA DEFINE POINTS
590 DATA SET DOMAIN,SET RANGE,SET X-AXIS SCALING
600 DATA SET Y-AXIS SCALING,DEFINE FUNCTION,DEFINE TITLES
610 DATA INITIATE GRAPHING
700 REM DEFINES (X,Y) POINTS
710 GOSUB 900:INPUT "HOW MANY POINTS";DP
720 PRINT "ENTER THESE";DP;"POINTS AS X,Y (ONE PAIR PER
    LINE)"
730 FOR J2=1 TO DP:INPUT X(J2),Y(J2):NEXT J2
740 PRINT "DONE ENTERING.":RETURN
880 FOR J=1 TO DP:POKE M(J),N(J):NEXT J:RETURN
890 REM LINE 900 CLEARS VIDEO SCREEN COMPLETELY
900 PRINT CHR$(12);:POKE -3968,32:RETURN
990 REM LINES 1000-1030 FOR POINTS NOT ON SCREEN
1000 M(J)=-3968:N(J)=32
1010 FOR K=1 TO 25
1020 POKE (K-2175),(ASC(MID$("SOME POINTS ARE OFF GRAPH",K,
     1)))
1030 NEXT K:RETURN
1190 REM LINES 1200-1240 PRINT BORDER OF GRAPH
1200 GOSUB 2500
1210 FOR J=0 TO 25:POKE (64*J-3966+ML),128:NEXT J
1220 POKE (ML-2366),156
1230 FOR J=1 TO (57-ML):POKE (ML+J-2366),176:NEXT J
1240 RETURN
1290 REM LINES 1300-1340 PRINT TITLES ON GRAPH
1300 K=ML-3940-INT(GT(0)/2)
1305 FOR J=1 TO GT(0):POKE (J+K),GT(J):NEXT J
1310 K=ML-2084-INT(AT(0)/2)
1315 FOR J=1 TO AT(0):POKE (J+K),AT(J):NEXT J
```

```
1320 K=-3200-64*INT(OT(0)/2)
1330 FOR J=1 TO OT(0):POKE (64*J+K),OT(J):NEXT J
1340 RETURN
1390 LINES 1400-1490 INPUT TITLES FOR GRAPH
1400 INPUT "GRAPH TITLE";Q$:GT(0)=LEN(Q$)
1410 IF GT(0)>50 THEN GT(0)=50
1420 FOR J=1 TO GT(0):GT(J)=ASC(MID$(Q$,J,1)):NEXT J
1430 INPUT "ABSCISSA TITLE";Q$:AT(0)=LEN(Q$)
1440 IF AT(0)>50 THEN AT(0)=50
1450 FOR J=1 TO AT(0):AT(J)=ASC(MID$(Q$,J,1)):NEXT J
1460 INPUT "ORDINATE TITLE";Q$:OT(0)=LEN(Q$)
1470 IF OT(0)>25 THEN OT(0)=25
1480 FOR J=1 TO OT(0):OT(J)=ASC(MID$(Q$,J,1)):NEXT J
1490 RETURN
1590 REM LINES 1600-1650 PRINT POINTS ON GRAPH
1600 GOSUB 900:GOSUB 2500:GOSUB 1200:GOSUB 2300:GOSUB 2400
1603 GOSUB 1300
1605 FOR J=1 TO DP:K=(54-ML)*(X(J)-XA)/(XB-XC)
1610 L=25*(Y(J)-YA)/(YB-YA)
1620 M(J)=64*(25-INT(L))-3966+ML+INT(K)
1630 N(J)=192+8*INT(8*(K-INT(K)))+INT(8*(L-INT(L)))
1640 IF M(J)<-3968 OR M(J)>-2305 THEN GOSUB 1000
1650 NEXT J:GOSUB 880:RETURN
1690 REM LINES 1700-1710 DEFINE POINTS
1700 FOR J=1 TO DP:X(J)=J*(XB-XA)/DP+XA
1710 Y(J)=FNA(X(J)):NEXT J:RETURN
2100 GOSUB 900
2110 INPUT "ENTER MINIMUM X, MAXIMUM X, AND INCREMENT";
     XA,XB,XC
2120 RETURN
2200 GOSUB 900
2210 INPUT "ENTER MINIMUM Y, MAXIMUM Y, AND INCREMENT";
     YA,YB,YC
2220 RETURN
2290 REM LINES 2300-2360 ARE X-AXIS SCALING
2300 GOSUB 2500:FOR J=XA TO XB STEP XC
2310 ZZ=(54-ML)*(J-XA)/(XB-XA):IF ZZ>(54-ML) THEN 2360
2315 ZB$=CHR$(128)+CHR$(129)+CHR$(130)+CHR$(131)+CHR$(162)
2316 ZB$=ZB$+CHR$(133)+CHR$(134)+CHR$(135)
2320 AA=ASC(MID$(ZB$,(1+INT(8*(ZZ-INT(ZZ)))),1))
2330 K=INT(ZZ)-2302+ML:POKE K,AA
2340 O$=STR$(J):L=LEN(Q$):FOR P=1 TO L
2350 POKE (K+P+63-INT(L/2)),(ASC(MID$(Q$,P,1))):NEXT P
2360 NEXT J:RETURN
2390 REM LINES 2400-2470 ARE Y-AXIS SCALING SUBROUTINE
2400 GOSUB 2500:FOR J=YA TO YB STEP YC
```

```
2410 ZZ=25*(J-YA)/(YB-YA):IF ZZ>25 THEN 2460
2415 ZA$=CHR$(176)+CHR$(175)+CHR$(174)+CHR$(151)+CHR$(140)
2416 ZA$=ZA$+CHR$(139)+CHR$(138)+CHR$(137)
2420 AA=ASC(MID$(ZA$,(1+INT(8*(ZZ-INT(ZZ)))),1))
2430 K=-64*INT(ZZ)-2367+ML:POKE K,AA
2440 Q$=STR$(J):L=LEN(Q$):FOR P=1 TO L
2450 POKE (K-L-1+P),(ASC(MID$(Q$,P,1)))
2460 NEXT P,J:RETURN
2490 REM LINES 2500-2520 GIVE WIDTH OF Y-SCALING
2500 ML=0:FOR J=YA TO YB STEP YC
2510 L=LEN(STR$(J)):IF L>ML THEN ML=L
2520 NEXT J:RETURN
2600 REM               DEFINE GRAPHIC CHARACTERS
2610 FOR J=-512 TO -1:POKE J,0:NEXT J
2620 V=128:N=-512
2630 FOR K=1 TO 8:FOR J=1 TO 8
2640 N=N+7:POKE N,V:NEXT J:N=N+8
2650 V=V/2:NEXT K:RETURN
3000 REM               INSTRUCTIONS FOR USE
3010 PRINT CHR$(12);
3015 PRINT "          INSTRUCTIONS FOR USE":PRINT
3020 PRINT"     First set the domain and the range."
3030 PRINT"This is for the X and Y axes. Make sure "
3040 PRINT"that the points will fall within the range"
3050 PRINT"and the domain or else you will get an"
3060 PRINT"?FC ERROR IN 1710 message or something to"
3070 PRINT"that effect."
3075 PRINT
3080 PRINT"     You may either define the points or"
3090 PRINT"have the computer do it using the function"
3100 PRINT"in line 15, which you can redefine. If you"
3110 PRINT"have the computer define the points, type"
3120 PRINT"DEFINE FUNCTION .If you choose to define"
3130 PRINT"the points yourself, you can enter each"
3140 PRINT"coordinate separately or enter X,Y pairs."
3145 PRINT
3150 PRINT"     Titles may be defined at any time."
3160 PRINT"Adjustments can be made to the X or Y "
3170 PRINT"axes by setting their scaling. Graphing"
3180 PRINT"is accomplished last by typing, "
3190 PRINT"INITIATE GRAPHING"
3200 PRINT:PRINT:PRINT
3210 INPUT "READY";AN$
3220 RETURN
4000 REM               FADE OUT TITLE
4005 FOR Z=1 TO 20
```

```
4020 FOR K=-625 TO -632 STEP -1
4025 J=2^(8*RND(1))+1
4030 POKE K,(255 AND J)
4040 NEXT K
4050 FOR I=1 TO 100:NEXT I
4060 NEXT Z:RETURN
5000 REM              SCREEN DUMP TO PRINTER
5005 DIM VA(30,60):FOR J=1 TO 30:FOR K=1 TO 60
5007 VA(J,K)=PEEK(64*(J-1)+K-3969):NEXT K,J
5010 N1=3*2^INT(6*RND(1))
5020 POKE 260,0:POKE 261,0:POKE 0,62:POKE 1,27
5030 POKE 2,205:POKE 3,12:POKE 4,224:POKE 5,201
5040 XX=USR(0):POKE 1,65:XX=USR(0):POKE 1,2:XX=USR(0)
5050 FOR J=1 TO 30:FOR L=-8 TO -1
5060 FOR K=0 TO 59:IF K/15=INT(K/15) THEN GOSUB 5100
5070 CN=PEEK(L-8*(255-VA(J,K+1))):FOR M=7 TO 0 STEP -1
5080 POKE 1,N1*SGN(CN AND 2^M):XX=USR(0):NEXT M,K
5090 POKE 1,13:XX=USR(0):NEXT L,J:POKE 1,12:XX=USR(0):RETURN
5100 POKE 1,27:XX=USR(0):POKE 1,75:XX=USR(0)
5110 POKE 1,120:XX=USR(0):POKE 1,0:XX=USR(0):RETURN
READY
```

Lines 3-7 give the name of the program and other information about it. Line 10 increases the available string space to 100. Line 15 defines a function. Line 20 sets the data points at 100. Lines 30-35 dimension arrays. GT is for the graph title; AT is for the abscissa title; OT is for the ordinate title. Line 40 clears the video screen. Line 50 contains three print statements for spacing down. Lines 60-270 are print and tab statements that contain graphic characters, which are printed as ones. Line 275 calls the subroutine at line 4000, which changes the graphic characters while they are on the screen, making them appear to sparkle. After three more print statements in line 280, line 285 asks if the user wants instructions. If the answer is yes, it calls the subroutine at line 3000. Line 287 calls the subroutine at line 2600, which defines graphic characters containing a dot in each of 64 possible positions. Line 290 calls the subroutine at line 500, which asks you to enter certain parameters, or ways that you want the result to be printed. Line 295 calls the subroutine at line 5000, which is a screen dump to the printer. Line 300 ends the program.

Lines 400-480 define the variable (if you want to enter them one number at a time). Lines 500-600 enter the graphing parameters. Some of the data is located in lines 580-610. Note the use of the restore statement in line 570. Lines 700-740 request you to enter the coordinates of the points you wish to plot. You must enter each X and Y as a pair. Line 880 is a subroutine that pokes the points onto the screen. Line 900 clears the video screen. Lines 990-1030 are used when you enter coordinates for points that will not appear on the screen. An error message is poked on the bottom line of the screen. Lines 1190-1240 print the border of the graph. Lines 1290-1340 print titles on the graph. Lines 1390-1490 allow you to input the titles for the graph. Lines 1590-1650 calculate the positions at which points must be printed on the graph. Lines 1690-1710 define the points when you are using the function in line 15. Lines 2110-2220 are for entering the scaling of the graph. Lines 2290-2360 are for the X-axis scaling. Lines 2390-2460 are for the Y-axis scaling. Lines 2490-2520 give the width of the Y-scaling. Lines 2600-2650 define special graphic characters that are represented as dots. Lines

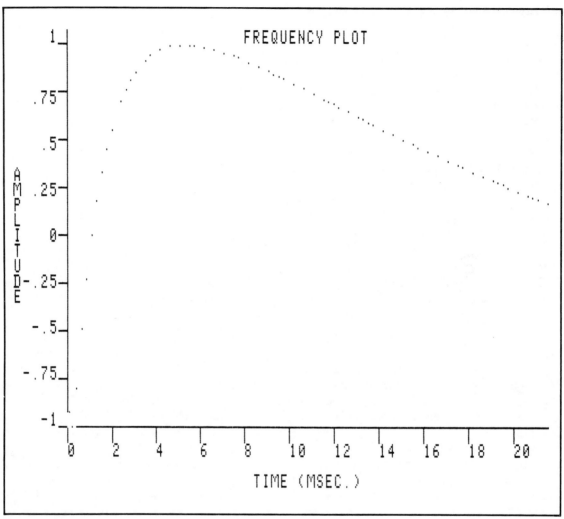

Fig. 5-2. A large-scale high-resolution data point plot.

3000-3220 give the instructions for use. The sub-routine in lines 4000-4060 fades out the title by changing the graphic characters on the screen. Lines 5000-5110 are an optional screen dump, which will enable you to print the graph.

As we have said, this program may not work on the many computers that do not allow you to define graphic characters.

A Function Plotter in BASIC—Program 13

The high-resolution function plotter that we discussed in Chapter 3 can be expanded so that each number in the array can represent more than the 12 points that it represented in that program. In this program we will attempt to have it represent up to 19 numbers. Since 8-bit microcomputers use up to 24 bits to represent the mantissa of a number and will typically hold an integer as large as six digits before it converts it to floating point notation, we have approached the practical limit of representing numbers as bits of another number in order to plot them as points. Since the Boolean algebra binary logical OR and AND functions may not work for such large numbers we have to split the number of bits in half and then do the logical operations on the two halves. The result is in Figure 5-3. The tattered appearance of the figure is due to rounding errors when such large numbers are added to such small numbers. The many manipulations necessary when erasing bits also contributes to the imprecise appearance. The method is nonetheless valid.

```
10 REM          3D HIGH RESOLUTION FUNCTION PLOTTER
20 REM                    SECOND VERSION
30 REM          WRITTEN BY TIMOTHY J. O'MALLEY
40 REM             COPYRIGHT 1982, TAB BOOKS INC.
50 REM
60 GOSUB 100:REM INITIALIZE PROGRAM
70 GOSUB 200:REM PLOT POINTS IN ARRAY
80 GOSUB 600:REM PRINT OUT ARRAY ON PAPER
90 END
100 REM              INITIALIZE PROGRAM
110 HGT=19:WID=349:W2=70
120 DEF FNA(R)=10*(EXP(-R*R/1000)*COS(R/6))
130 DIM VA(HGT,WID):REM DIMENSION ARRAY FOR PLOT
140 DIM A1(20):K=1
150 FOR J=0 TO 20:A1(J)=K:K=K*2:NEXT J:RETURN
200 REM            PLOT POINTS IN ARRAY
210 FOR X=-40 TO 40 STEP 0.5:FOR Y=-40 TO 40 STEP 0.2
220 R=SQR(X*X+Y*Y):Z=FNA(R):V=Y*0.17-X*0.08+Z+HGT/2
230 H=X*2.88+Y*2.61+WID/2:IF V<0 OR V>HGT OR H<0 OR
    H>WIDTHEN290
240 IV=INT(V):IH=INT(H):DV=INT(19*(V-IV)):PV=A1(DV)
250 IF (VA(IV,IH)>512) OR (PV>512) THEN GOSUB 300:GOTO 270
260 VA(IV,IH)=VA(IV,IH) OR PV
270 GOSUB 400:REM ERASE POINTS BELOW PV IN VA(IV,IH)
280 GOSUB 500:REM ERASE POINTS BELOW VA(IV,IH)
290 NEXT Y,X:RETURN
300 REM              NUMBERS TOO LARGE FOR OR FUNCTION
305 YS=INT(VA(IV,IH)/512):XS=VA(IV,IH)-512*YS
310 IF PV>512 THEN ZS=INT(PV/512):YS=YS OR ZS
320 IF PV<=512 THEN XS=XS OR PV
330 VA(IV,IH)=XS+512*YS:RETURN
350 REM              NUMBERS TOO LARGE FOR AND FUNCTION
360 YS=INT(VA(IV,IH)/512):XS=VA(IV,IH)-512*YS
370 IF J2>512 THEN ZS=INT(J2/512):IF (YSANDZS)=ZS THEN
    YS=YS-ZS
380 IF J2<=512 THEN IF (XS AND J2)=J2 THEN XS=XS-J2
390 VA(IV,IH)=XS+512*YS:RETURN
400 REM              ERASE POINTS BELOW PV IN VA(IV,IH)
410 IF DV=0 THEN RETURN
420 FOR J=DV-1 TO 0 STEP -1:J2=A1(J)
430 IF (J2>512) OR (VA(IV,IH)>512) THEN GOSUB 350:GOTO 450
```

```
440 IF (VA(IV,IH) AND J2)=J2 THEN VA(IV,IH)=VA(IV,IH)-J2
450 NEXT J:RETURN
500 REM              ERASE POINTS BELOW VA(IV,IH)
510 IF IV=0 THEN RETURN
520 FOR J=IV-1 TO 0 STEP -1:VA(J,IH)=0:NEXT J:RETURN
600 REM             PRINT OUT ARRAY ON PAPER
605 GOSUB 700:REM SET UP MACHINE LANGUAGE SUBROUTINE FOR
    PRINTER
610 FOR JS=HGT TO 0 STEP -1:FOR MS=18 TO 0 STEP -1
620 BS=A1(MS):FOR LS=0 TO 4:GOSUB 660
625 FOR KS=LS*W2 TO LS*W2+W2-1
630 IF (BS>512) OR (VA(JS,KS)>512) THEN GOSUB 800:GOTO 640
635 POKE 1,SGN(BS AND VA(JS,KS)):XX=USR(0)
640 NEXT KS,LS:POKE 1,13:XX=USR(0):NEXT MS,JS
650 POKE 1,12:XX=USR(0):RETURN
660 POKE 1,27:XX=USR(0):POKE 1,75:XX=USR(0):POKE 1,W2
670 XX=USR(0):POKE 1,0:XX=USR(0):RETURN
700 REM   SET UP MACHINE LANGUAGE SUBROUTINE FOR PRINTER
710 POKE 260,0:POKE 261,0:POKE 0,62:POKE 1,27:POKE 2,205
720 POKE 3,12:POKE 4,224:POKE 5,201:XX=USR(0):POKE 1,65
730 XX=USR(0):POKE 1,1:XX=USR(0):RETURN
800 REM    NUMBERS TOO LARGE FOR AND FUNCTION WHEN PRINTING
810 RS=0:YS=INT(VA(JS,KS)/512):XS=VA(JS,KS)-512*YS
820 IF BS>512 THEN ZS=INT(BS/512):IF (YS AND ZS)=ZS THEN RS=1
830 IF BS<=512 THEN IF (XS AND BS)=BS THEN RS=1
840 POKE 1,RS:XX=USR(0):RETURN
READY
```

Let's examine the program. Lines 10-50 give the name of the program and the other credits. Line 60 calls the subroutine that initializes the program. Line 70 plots points in the array. Line 80 prints out the points on paper using high-resolution graphics. Line 90 ends the program.

Line 100 is the remark statement for the initialization subroutine found in lines 100-150. Line 110 sets the height, width, and the variable W2 for the printer. Line 120 defines a function. Lines 130 and 140 dimension arrays and set the variable K to 1. Line 150 stores the powers of 2 in an array called A1. Then program control returns to line 70.

The points are plotted in lines 200-290 with line 200 being the remark statement which contains the subroutine's heading. In line 210 we have the start of two nested for-next loops that give the X and Y-coordinates. In line 220 R is set as the dis-

tance from the middle of the plot. Z is a function of this distance. In this program if the number PV or VA(IV,IH) is greater than 512 (2 to the power of 9), the numbers are too large for the OR function and the AND function, and they are split in two (not divided by two). Then the binary logical operations can be executed to plot the points. Lines 270 and 280 erase points below the most recently plotted point.

Lines 300-330 are the lines of the subroutine which split the numbers for the OR function. Lines 350-390 are the lines of the AND function subroutine which split the numbers that are too large. Lines 400-450 erase the bits in the number below the present bit position. Lines 500-520 erase the bits in the numbers below the current number by setting those numbers in the same column of the VA array to zero. Lines 600-670 form a machine-

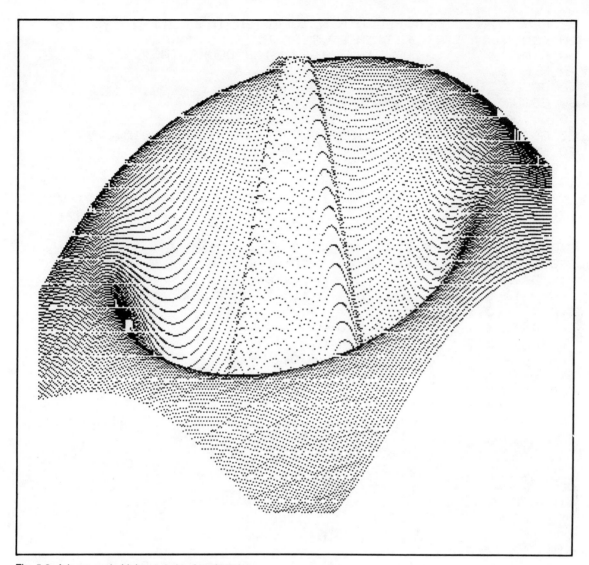

Fig. 5-3. A large-scale high-resolution function plot.

language utilizing subroutine that sends numbers to the printer, set up by the subroutine in lines 700-720. If the numbers are too large for the AND function used in the printing subroutine, the subroutine in lines 800-840 is used.

THREE-DIMENSIONAL SOLID FIGURE PLOTTERS

We now look at two programs that eliminate lines to make three-dimensional solid figures. These two programs use different techniques to eliminate hidden lines. We have already seen a couple of methods of eliminating points; namely, erasing points that are below the points plotted on a function, and sorting and ignoring points in the case of the molecular models.

An Architectural Drawing in BASIC—Program 14

Figure 5-4 shows one of the possible views of a simple solid figure in the shape of a building. This low-resolution figure is also in perspective.

```
10 REM            THREE DIMENSIONAL SOLID PLOTTER
20 REM            WRITTEN BY TIMOTHY J. O'MALLEY
30 REM            COPYRIGHT 1982, TAB BOOKS INC.
40 REM
50 GOSUB 200:REM INITIALIZE VARIABLES
60 GOSUB 500:REM BLANK ARRAY
70 GOSUB 600:REM ROTATE POINTS ABOUT AXIS
80 GOSUB 800:REM PLOT LINES AND ERASE HIDDEN POINTS
90 GOSUB 2000:REM PRINT OUT ARRAY
100 GOTO 60
200 REM          INITIALIZE VARIABLES
210 IP=10:IA=7:B$="Z":E=0.3:S=1:T=IP:F=0.1:G=0.98:U=31:W=63
220 DIM X(IP),Y(IP),Z(IP),R(3),VA(U,W),LL(IA,10),DI(IA),
    ST(IA)
230 FOR J=1 TO IP:READ X(J),Y(J),Z(J):NEXT J
240 FOR J=1 TO IA:FOR K=0 TO 10:READ LL(J,K):NEXT K,J
250 DATA 0,0,0, 0,1,0, 2,1,0, 2,0,0
260 DATA 0,0,1, 2,0,1, 0,0.5,1.5, 2,0.5,1.5
270 DATA 0,1,1, 2,1,1
280 DATA 5,1,2,3,4,1,0,0,0,0,0
290 DATA 5,1,5,6,4,1,0,0,0,0,0
300 DATA 5,3,10,9,2,3,0,0,0,0,0
310 DATA 5,5,6,8,7,5,0,0,0,0,0
320 DATA 5,8,10,9,7,8,0,0,0,0,0
330 DATA 6,1,2,9,7,5,1,0,0,0,0
340 DATA 6,4,3,10,8,6,4,0,0,0,0
350 R(1)=1:R(2)=0.5:R(3)=1
360 X(0)=1:Y(0)=-10:Z(0)=0.7
370 RETURN
500 REM              BLANK ARRAY
510 FOR J=0 TO U:FOR K=0 TO W:VA(J,K)=32:NEXT K,J
520 RETURN
600 REM              ROTATE POINTS ABOUT AXIS
610 FOR J=S TO T
620 IF B$="Z" THEN A1=X(J):A2=R(1):A3=Y(J):A4=R(2)
630 IF B$="Y" THEN A1=X(J):A2=R(1):A3=Z(J):A4=R(3)
640 IF B$="X" THEN A1=Y(J):A2=R(2):A3=Z(J):A4=R(3)
650 P1=A1-A2:P2=A3-A4
660 L=SQR(P1*P1+P2*P2)
670 IF P2=0 THEN A5=-(P1<0)*3.141593
680 IF P1=0 THEN A5=SGN(P2)*1.570796
690 IF P2<>0 AND P1<>0 THEN A5=ATN(P2/P1)-(P1<0)*3.141593
700 A5=A5+E
710 IF B$="Z" THEN X(J)=L*COS(A5)+R(1):Y(J)=L*SIN(A5)+R(2)
720 IF B$="Y" THEN X(J)=L*COS(A5)+R(1):Z(J)=L*SIN(A5)+R(3)
730 IF B$="X" THEN Y(J)=L*COS(A5)+R(2):Z(J)=L*SIN(A5)+R(3)
```

```
740 NEXT J
750 RETURN
800 REM              PLOT LINES AND ERASE HIDDEN POINTS
805 REM   LINES 810-840 FIND MEAN DISTANCES TO FACES
810 FOR J=1 TO IA:K=LL(J,0)-1:DI(J)=0
820 FOR L=1 TO K:SUM=(X(LL(J,L))-X(0))^2+(Y(LL(J,L))-Y(0))^2
830 DI(J)=DI(J)+SQR(SUM+(Z(LL(J,L))-Z(0))^2)
840 NEXT L:DI(J)=DI(J)/K:ST(J)=J:NEXT J
850 REM LINES 860-940 ARE A DESCENDING ARRAY SORTER FOR ST
860 FOR J=1 TO IA-1
870 K=J
880 IF DI(K)>=DI(K+1) THEN 940
890 A=ST(K):B=DI(K)
900 ST(K)=ST(K+1):DI(K)=DI(K+1)
910 ST(K+1)=A:DI(K+1)=B
920 K=K-1
930 IF K>0 THEN 880
940 NEXT J
945 REM   CONVERT X,Y,Z TO H,V  (LINES 950-1150)
950 FOR J=1 TO IP
960 DY=Y(J)-Y(0):IF DY<=0 THEN PRINT "DECREASE Y(0)":STOP
970 DX=X(J)-X(0)
980 DZ=Z(J)-Z(0)
990 V(J)=ATN(F*DZ/DY)
1000 H(J)=ATN(F*DX/DY)
1010 NEXT J
1020 MINV=V(1):MAXV=V(1)
1030 MINH=H(1):MAXH=H(1)
1040 FOR J=1 TO IP
1050 IF V(J)<MINV THEN MINV=V(J)
1060 IF V(J)>MAXV THEN MAXV=V(J)
1070 IF H(J)<MINH THEN MINH=H(J)
1080 IF H(J)>MAXH THEN MAXH=H(J)
1090 NEXT J
1100 DH=MAXH-MINH
1110 DV=MAXV-MINV
1120 FOR J=1 TO IP
1130 H(J)=G*(H(J)-MINH)/DH*W
1140 V(J)=G*(V(J)-MINV)/DV*U
1150 NEXT J
1155 REM LINES 1160-1670 DRAW LINES, PLOT, AND ERASE POINTS
1160 FOR L=1 TO IA
1170 FOR J=1 TO LL(ST(L),0)-1
1180 HH=H(LL(ST(L),J+1))-H(LL(ST(L),J))
1190 VV=V(LL(ST(L),J+1))-V(LL(ST(L),J))
1210 IF HH=0 THEN 1310
```

```
1220 M=VV/HH
1230 B=V(LL(ST(L),J))-M*H(LL(ST(L),J))
1240 SP=SQR(VV*VV+HH*HH)
1250 FOR K=H(LL(ST(L),J)) TO H(LL(ST(L),J+1)) STEP HH/SP
1260 P=M*K+B
1270 GOSUB 1400
1280 NEXT K
1290 NEXT J
1300 GOTO 1440
1310 REM                SLOPE EQUALS INFINITY
1320 K=H(LL(ST(L),J))
1330 IF VV=0 THEN P=V(LL(ST(L),J)):GOSUB 1400:GOTO 1290
1340 FOR P=V(LL(ST(L),J)) TO V(LL(ST(L),J+1)) STEP SGN(VV)
1350 GOSUB 1400
1360 NEXT P:GOTO 1290
1400 REM                PLOTTING SUBROUTINE
1410 IF P>U OR P<0 OR K>W OR K<0 THEN RETURN
1420 V1=INT(P):V2=INT(K)
1430 VA(V1,V2)=40:RETURN
1440 MPV=0:MPH=0
1450 FOR J=1 TO LL(ST(L),0)-1
1460 MPV=V(LL(ST(L),J))+MPV:MPH=H(LL(ST(L),J))+MPH
1470 NEXT J:MPV=INT(MPV/(LL(ST(L),0)-1))
1480 MPH=INT(MPH/(LL(ST(L),0)-1))
1495 REM LINES 1500-1620 ERASE POINTS WITHIN POLYGON FACE
1500 ML=SQR(W*W+U*U)
1510 FOR J=0 TO 6.3 STEP 0.02:K=0
1520 HI=MPH+INT(K*COS(J)):VI=MPV+INT(K*SIN(J))
1525 IF K>ML OR VI>U OR VI<0 OR HI>W OR HI<0 THEN 1620
1530 IF VA(VI,HI)=40 THEN 1620
1540 VA(VI,HI)=32
1550 K=K+0.4
1560 GOTO 1520
1620 NEXT J
1625 REM LINES 1630-1660 CHANGE MARKER CHARACTERS TO
     ASTERISKS
1630 FOR J=0 TO U:FOR K=0 TO W
1650 IF VA(J,K)=40 THEN VA(J,K)=42
1660 NEXT K,J
1670 NEXT L:RETURN
2000 REM                PRINT OUT ARRAY
2010 FOR J=U TO 0 STEP -1
2020 FOR K=0 TO W
2030 PRINT CHR$(VA(J,K));
2040 NEXT K
2050 PRINT
```

```
2060 NEXT J
2070 PRINT CHR$(12);
2080 RETURN
READY
```

Let's quickly run through the program to see how we eliminated the hidden points. Lines 10-40 give the credits. Line 50 calls the subroutine at line 200, which sets up the variables, dimensions the arrays, and reads data, etc. Line 60 blanks the array that is used to store the points by calling the subroutine at line 500. Line 70 calls the subroutine at line 600, which rotates the points. Line 80 calls the subroutine at line 800, which plots the lines and erases the hidden points. Line 90 prints out the array of points. Line 100 directs control to line 60 to make an endless loop to present all the different views of the model.

In the subroutine in lines 200-370, IP is the number of points used to determine the figure. IA is the number of polygon sides or faces on the figure.

The other variables are the same as in other programs. The LL array is a linked list of line connections for the polygon sides. Each line (row) of the array is the connection for a side. The first number in each row of the array is used to tell the number of line connections for each side. The remaining numbers in the array indicate the number of the point used, much like in other programs.

Line 500 sets all the array elements of VA to 32, the ASCII code for the blank space. Lines 600-750 rotate points exactly as in earlier programs. Lines 810-840 find the mean (average) distance to each polygon face. This information is used to determine what face to plot first, second and so forth. We plot the face furthest from the viewpoint first. Lines 860-940 sort the indices of the points by

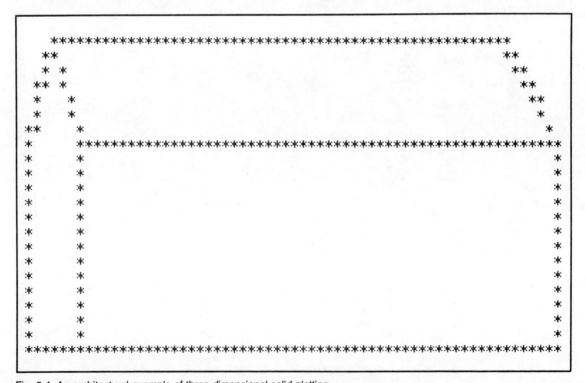

Fig. 5-4. An architectural example of three-dimensional solid plotting.

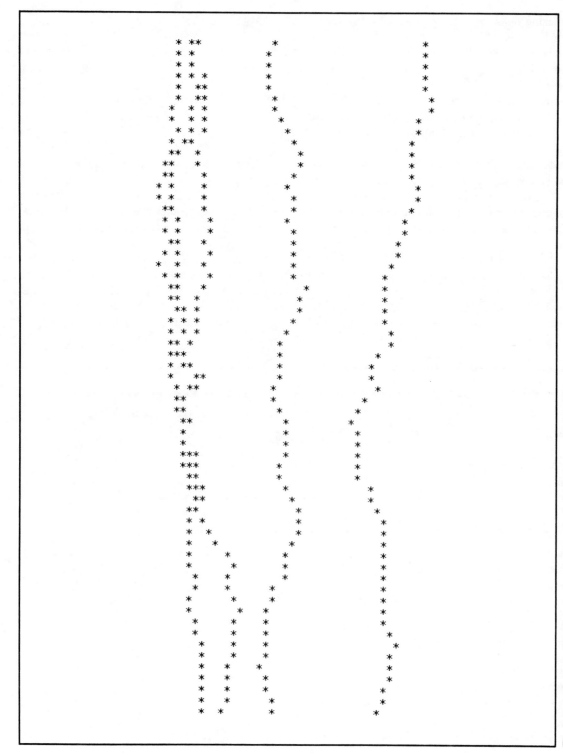

Fig. 5-5. A landscape profile, another example of three-dimensional solid plotting.

decreasing distances of the faces from the viewpoint. Lines 950-1150 convert the X, Y, Z coordinates of the points to horizontal and vertical values much like in earlier subroutines that plotted perspective lines. Here we complicate things a little by making use of the linked list.

In line 1440, MPV is the vertical value of the midpoint of the polygon side, and MPH is the horizontal value of that midpoint. We set it to zero initially, and then find its true value in lines 1450-1480. Lines 1500-1620 erase points within each polygon side. It changes the value of anything near

A Landscape in BASIC—Program 15

Figure 5-5 depicts an artificial landscape made by a computer and a printer. It resembles a rocky terrain in which the valleys in the background are hidden by the peaks in the foreground. Since this program uses the random (RND) function, this figure is only one of many that are possible.

The program is fairly simple. Lines 10-40 give the credits. Line 50 sets the height of the printout at 60, and sets W, the number of ridges in the figure, to six. Line 60 dimensions the VA array to those values. The nested loop in lines 70-100 determines the values of the points in the array using the RND

```
10 REM           NATURAL SCENE (BROWNIAN GENERATION)
20 REM               WRITTEN BY TIMOTHY J. O'MALLEY
30 REM               COPYRIGHT 1982, TAB BOOKS INC.
40 REM
50 U=60:W=6
60 DIM VA(U,W)
70 FOR H=1 TO W
75 VA(0,H)=15+H*7*RND(1)
80 FOR V=1 TO U
90 VA(V,H)=VA(V-1,H)+(RND(1)-0.5)*4*RND(1)
100 NEXT V,H
110 FOR V=0 TO U
120 P=0
130 FOR H=0 TO W
140 I=VA(V,H)
150 IF I<=P OR I>63 THEN 180
160 PRINT TAB(I);"*";
170 P=I
180 NEXT H:PRINT:NEXT V
READY
```

the midpoint to 32. Lines 1630-1660 change the number 40 in the array to 42, the ASCII code for the asterisk. We used the number 40 to indicate the boundary of the polygon, a number that would not be erased by the program. See line 1530. Lines 2000-2080 print out the array as characters, either blanks or asterisks.

function. Lines 110-180 print out the figures. Line 150 says if a value position of a point is to the left of the last points, that is hidden, go to the next point. This corresponds to a valley in the figure.

This program uses so-called Brownian generation because each point is determined in part by the position of the last point in the same ridge.

Chapter 6

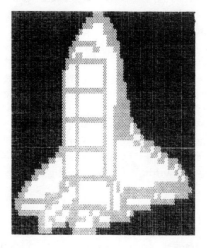

Computer Art

The video display screen and printer of the personal computer may be used for many purposes; among them is computer art. Imagine! Think of all the possible images that can be created and displayed on the screen or on paper. Any image that can be made as a pattern of light and dark points, and in some cases, colored points can be generated by the personal computer.

Let's look at some of the ways of producing the images that comprise computer art. Remember that the imagination of the programmer and the sophistication of his system determine the quality of the computer-produced art.

HOW TO GENERATE COMPUTER ART

It all starts with an idea. A programmer has an idea which he wants to turn into a work of art to display using the computer. He can approach it in at least two ways: he can sketch the work on graph paper and then transfer the points to the computer for precise definition and positioning; or he can have the computer define all the points mathemati-

cally, according to some algorithm. He might then refine the image by deleting some points to highlight a particular feature. When finished, he has a work of computer art.

Handmade Method

Let's examine each of these methods in detail. In the handmade method, you might start with a photograph or drawing of a subject of interest. Since points lie in specific positions, graph paper can be used to specify their locations. Squares containing points would be filled in. If a line ran through a square on a graph paper, the square could be filled in.

In a method called simple thresholding, a square of the graph paper would be filled in if a line ran through that square or if, in the case of shading, that square corresponded to an area that was darkened. In partially shaded squares it would be filled if the square was 50% (or more) filled. Each picture element would be transferred until the entire image was completed. A more complex method would be to assign values, of for example, zero to nine, to each picture element and then to use colored dots ranging from a bright color to a dark color as the values ranged from zero to nine. This process would be very tedious and may not be worth the time because there are better alternatives.

The handmade method is good for defining still images especially still components. A still image is a large picture that is intended to be displayed once. It can't be manipulated easily and will occupy the same part of the video screen each time that it is displayed. A still component is a small portion of that image that can be moved about on the video display.

Computer-Generated Method

Computer-generated art does not require the nitty-gritty kind of labor that the handmade method demands. Software is used exclusively to synthesize a picture. To make the picture, the computer would run through a program and decide what picture elements to turn "on" or leave "off". It might also be programmed to alter the image to create an abstraction, an exaggeration of reality.

To make a circle, for instance, the computer would use the equation of a circle to plot points. Squares, triangles, and other figures might also be plotted from their mathematical definitions. Various techniques might be used to generate altered images: simple figures could be distorted by some factor; false colors might be applied to perform highlighting.

STILL IMAGES

We will now direct our attention to the making of a still image using the handmade method. We will look at two types of graphic characters.

As we said earlier, some computers use graphic characters that have ASCII codes above 128. To print these characters, the programmer simply types: PRINT CHR$(N), where N is the code number for the graphic character. The programmer might supply the values for N in data statements in the handmade method. The program would contain a series of data statements containing the location of points that the computer would read in the print as graphic characters.

Other computers allow you to activate individual dots or rectangles on the video display screen. Some of these computers use a function called set, where (SET(X,Y) would turn "on" the rectangle at position (X,Y) on the video screen. The programmer need only supply a list of coordinates and have the computer perform a series of sets to display the image on the screen. Other computers that activate individual dots turn "on" the points by altering the bits of the memory location that relate to the screen RAM.

The Space Shuttle As An Example—Program 16

Figure 6-1 is the image of the space shuttle made using the handmade method. In this case we drew the shuttle on graph paper, filled in squares that were dark areas, then calculated the numbers that resulted if we assumed that the dark areas were bits of a number. That is, using groups of eight positions, if the rightmost square is the only one that is darkened, the number is 1. If the leftmost square is darkened, the number is 128. Thus we take the binary of the squares and make decimal numbers. We present the BASIC program that made the figure but we will not examine it in detail.

```
10 REM              HIGH RESOLUTION REALISTIC ART
20 REM              WRITTEN BY TIMOTHY J. O'MALLEY
30 REM              COPYRIGHT 1982, TAB BOOKS INC.
40 REM
45 PRINT CHR$(12);:REM CLEAR SCREEN (SOME USE CLS)
50 GOSUB 1000:REM   DEFINE GRAPHICS
60 GOSUB 2000:REM   PLACE GRAPHICS ON SCREEN
190 END
200 DATA 88
```

```
210 DATA 24,0,1,3,7,7,15,14,30,112,252,246,143,248,0,0,31
220 DATA 0,0,0,0,128,192,32,160
230 DATA 104
240 DATA 24,31,56,32,32,33,33,97,97,43,48,0,0,255,0,0,0
250 DATA 208,24,8,228,252,66,66,66
260 DATA 96
270 DATA 32,0,0,0,1,1,1,3,3,97,225,225,225,225,225,225,225
280 DATA 0,0,0,255,0,0,0,0,66,66,66,253,66,66,66,66
290 DATA 96
300 DATA 32,3,7,7,11,11,19,35,68,241,241,241,241,241,241,241
    ,17
310 DATA 0,0,255,0,0,0,0,0,66,66,252,66,66,66,66,66
320 DATA 80
330 DATA 64,0,0,0,0,3,12,19,36,1,6,27,108,176,192,0,0
340 DATA 152,224,0,0,0,0,0,0,17,17,17,17,17,33,33,33
350 DATA 0,255,0,0,0,0,0,0,66,254,71,66,66,66,66,66
360 DATA 0,0,128,192,48,24,6,3,0,0,0,0,0,0,0,128
370 DATA 64
380 DATA 64,72,96,112,255,135,224,31,0,0,0,0,255,255,35,160
    ,126
390 DATA 0,0,0,0,254,255,3,3,35,38,36,36,40,232,200,200
400 DATA 255,0,0,0,0,0,0,0,254,126,115,92,70,67,65,64
410 DATA 0,0,0,128,96,96,255,127,224,112,28,14,6,3,255,255
420 DATA 72
430 DATA 56,1,0,0,0,0,0,0,0,243,13,5,5,3,3,0,0
440 DATA 201,217,254,248,240,255,127,1,255,152,136,248,31,247
450 DATA 248,255,216,87,49,24,247,224,192,128,28,12,199,54
460 DATA 142,102,30,0,3,30,224,0,0,0,0,0
470 DATA 128
1000 REM              DEFINE GRAPHICS
1010 A=-1025:M=0
1020 FOR J=1 TO 15:READ Z:N=0
1030 FOR K=1 TO Z:A=A+1:IF M<0 THEN READ N
1040 POKE A,N:NEXT K:M=NOT(M):NEXT J
1050 RETURN
2000 REM              PLACE GRAPHICS ON SCREEN
2010 FOR Q=192 TO 1216 STEP 512
2020 FOR P=Q-3968 TO Q-3920 STEP 16
2030 L=127
2040 FOR J=P TO P+511 STEP 64
2050 FOR K=0 TO 15
2060 L=L+1
2070 POKE (J+K),L
2080 NEXT K,J,P,Q
2090 RETURN
READY
```

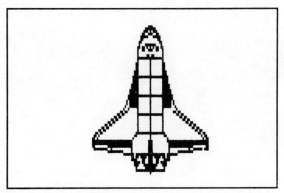

Fig. 6-1. Top view of space shuttle created using the hand-made method.

tronic units, or even plumbing parts. They can be arranged on the video screen according to your wishes. The ease with which they can be manipulated makes them valuable for images with moving parts.

The numbers that define each component are stored as an array under a variable name. When that component is needed, the computer locates the correct position on the screen and then uses the numbers from the array to print the still component on the video display.

Advantages and Disadvantages of Still Images

Still images are good if they are to be used once and do not need to be manipulated in any way. Still images would be good for file purposes. Perhaps you want to store a picture on tape or disk for retrieval at a later date. Still images would be good for that purpose. Should you want to manipulate the still image, you would be at a disadvantage; still images are not easily moved.

STILL COMPONENTS: MOVABLE UNITS OF STILL IMAGES

One way to manipulate still images is to divide those stills into components and then move the components. By taking small blocks, you can manage the images fairly easily.

If your computer is capable of defining graphic characters, you can create specific still components. These components can be whatever you need: electrical symbols for wiring diagrams, elec-

Chessmen as an Example—Programs 17 and 18

Figure 6-2 is the display of a chessboard and Fig. 6-3 is a display of a chessboard with chess pieces on it. A chess game is a pefect example of the use of still components: the men have to be moved about on the screen, and the programmer can define the way the men are made to suit his personal wishes. The chess program that uses the pieces would control where the pieces are placed during the course of the game.

We will not look at how we defined the chessboard or the chessmen, but we will present the BASIC programs that created them. Each dark square on the chessboard was made of eight rectangular graphic characters in a 2×4 array. Each chessman was made of a 2×2 array of four graphic characters that were defined by numbers in data statements. Since squares were either white or black, we had to make two sets of men: one for use on white squares and one for use on black squares. The men occupy the center of each square. You can, of course, change the way the chessmen appear by redefining them.

```
10 REM               CHESSBOARD AND SCREEN DUMP
20 REM            WRITTEN BY TIMOTHY J. O'MALLEY
30 REM             COPYRIGHT 1982, TAB BOOKS INC.
40 REM
50 REM               PRINT CHESSBOARD ON SCREEN
60 PRINT CHR$(12);:P=-3892:L=-1
70 FOR J=0 TO 31:P=P+1:POKE P,176:NEXT J:P=P+1
80 FOR J=1 TO 8:FOR M=1 TO 2:P=P+31:POKE P,135
90 FOR K=1 TO 8:FOR N=1 TO 4:P=P+1:POKE P,(177+145*L)
100 NEXT N:L=NOT L:NEXT K:L=NOT L:P=P+1:POKE P,128
```

```
110 L=NOT L:NEXT M:L=NOT L:NEXT J:P=P+31
120 FOR J=1 TO 32:P=P+1:POKE P,137:NEXT J
200 REM            SCREEN DUMP TO PRINTER
210 N1=3*2^INT(6*RND(1))
220 POKE 260,0:POKE 261,0:POKE 0,62:POKE 1,27
230 POKE 2,205:POKE 3,12:POKE 4,224:POKE 5,201
240 X=USR(0):POKE 1,65:X=USR(0):POKE 1,2:X=USR(0)
250 FOR J=1 TO 29:C1=64*J-3968:FOR L=-8 TO -1
260 FOR K=0 TO 59:IF K/15=INT(K/15) THEN GOSUB 300
270 CN=PEEK(L-8*(255-PEEK(C1+K))):FOR M=7 TO 0 STEP -1
280 POKE 1,N1*SGN(CN AND 2^M):X=USR(0):NEXT M,K
290 POKE 1,13:X=USR(0):NEXT L,J:POKE 1,12:X=USR(0):RETURN
300 POKE 1,27:X=USR(0):POKE 1,75:X=USR(0)
310 POKE 1,120:X=USR(0):POKE 1,0:X=USR(0):RETURN
READY


10 REM             CHESSBOARD AND SCREEN DUMP
20 REM            WRITTEN BY TIMOTHY J. O'MALLEY
30 REM             COPYRIGHT 1982, TAB BOOKS INC.
40 REM
45 REM            CLEAR SCREEN
50 PRINT CHR$(12);
51 DIM BD(8,8)
52 FOR J=1 TO 2:FOR K=1 TO 8:READ BD(J,K):NEXT K,J
53 FOR J=7 TO 8:FOR K=1 TO 8:READ BD(J,K):NEXT K,J
54 DATA 200,232,204,220,192,228,208,224
55 DATA 236,212,236,212,236,212,236,212
56 DATA 148,172,148,172,148,172,148,172
57 DATA 160,144,164,132,152,140,168,136
59 REM             READ IN GRAPHICS
60 P=-3892:L=-1:P1=P+66
61 FOR J=-1024 TO -601:READ N:POKE J,N:NEXT J
62 FOR J=-512 TO -129:READ N:POKE J,N:NEXT J
69 REM             DRAW CHESSBOARD
70 FOR J=0 TO 31:P=P+1:POKE P,180:NEXT J:P=P+1
80 FOR J=1 TO 8:FOR M=1 TO 2:P=P+31:POKE P,176
90 FOR K=1 TO 8:FOR N=1 TO 4:P=P+1:POKE P,(177+145*L)
100 NEXT N:L=NOT L:NEXT K:L=NOT L:P=P+1:POKE P,178
110 L=NOT L:NEXT M:L=NOT L:NEXT J:P=P+31
120 FOR J=1 TO 32:P=P+1:POKE P,179:NEXT J
121 REM            PLACE MEN ON BOARD
122 FOR J=1 TO 8:Z1=P1+128*(J-1)
123 FOR K=1 TO 8:Z=Z1+4*(K-1)
124 IF BD(J,K)=0 THEN 127
125 POKE Z,BD(J,K):POKE Z+1,BD(J,K)+1
126 POKE Z+64,BD(J,K)+2:POKE Z+65,BD(J,K)+3
```

```
127 NEXT K,J
128 DATA 0,1,7,1,15,4,2,14
129 DATA 0,128,224,128,240,32,64,112
130 DATA 2,2,2,4,24,32,63,0
131 DATA 64,64,64,32,24,4,252,0
132 DATA 0,1,15,4,2,14,4,2
133 DATA 0,128,240,32,64,112,32,64
134 DATA 2,2,2,4,24,32,63,0
135 DATA 64,64,64,32,24,4,252,0
136 DATA 0,0,13,13,15,4,4,4
137 DATA 0,0,176,176,240,32,32,32
138 DATA 4,4,4,4,8,16,31,0
139 DATA 32,32,32,32,16,8,248,0
140 DATA 0,1,2,4,2,14,2,2
141 DATA 0,128,64,32,64,112,64,64
142 DATA 2,2,2,4,8,16,31,0
143 DATA 64,64,64,32,16,8,248,0
144 DATA 0,0,0,3,12,55,57,2
145 DATA 0,0,192,48,8,4,4,4
146 DATA 4,8,8,4,8,16,31,0
147 DATA 8,16,16,32,16,8,248,0
148 DATA 0,0,0,0,3,4,4,2
149 DATA 0,0,0,0,192,32,32,64
150 DATA 14,2,2,4,8,16,31,0
151 DATA 112,64,64,32,16,8,248,0
152 DATA 85,169,87,161,79,164,82,174
153 DATA 85,138,229,138,245,42,69,114
154 DATA 82,170,82,164,88,160,63,170
155 DATA 69,74,85,42,25,4,253,170
156 DATA 85,161,79,164,82,174,68,162
157 DATA 85,130,245,42,69,114,37,74
158 DATA 82,170,82,164,88,160,63,170
159 DATA 85,74,69,34,25,4,253,170
160 DATA 85,170,77,173,79,164,68,164
161 DATA 85,170,181,178,245,42,37,42
162 DATA 68,164,68,164,72,144,95,170
163 DATA 37,42,37,42,21,10,249,170
164 DATA 85,171,86,172,82,174,66,162
165 DATA 85,170,85,42,69,122,69,74
166 DATA 82,162,82,164,72,144,95,170
167 DATA 85,74,85,42,21,10,249,170
168 DATA 85,170,84,163,76,183,57,130
169 DATA 85,42,197,50,9,4,5,4
170 DATA 68,168,88,164,72,144,95,170
171 DATA 9,26,37,34,21,10,249,170
172 DATA 85,170,85,168,83,164,84,162
```

```
173 DATA 85,170,85,10,197,42,37,74
174 DATA 78,162,82,164,72,144,95,170
175 DATA 117,74,69,34,17,10,249,170
176 DATA 1,1,1,1,1,1,1,1
177 DATA 85,170,85,170,85,170,85,170
178 DATA 128,128,128,128,128,128,128,128
179 DATA 255,0,0,0,0,0,0,0
180 DATA 0,0,0,0,0,0,0,255
200 REM            SCREEN DUMP TO PRINTER
210 N1=3*2^INT(6*RND(1))
220 POKE 260,0:POKE 261,0:POKE 0,62:POKE 1,27
230 POKE 2,205:POKE 3,12:POKE 4,224:POKE 5,201
240 X=USR(0):POKE 1,65:X=USR(0):POKE 1,2:X=USR(0)
250 FOR J=1 TO 29:C1=64*J-3968:FOR L=-8 TO -1
260 FOR K=0 TO 59:IF K/15=INT(K/15) THEN GOSUB 300
270 CN=PEEK(L-8*(255-PEEK(C1+K))):FOR M=7 TO 0 STEP -1
280 POKE 1,N1*SGN(CN AND 2^M):X=USR(0):NEXT M,K
290 POKE 1,13:X=USR(0):NEXT L,J:POKE 1,12:X=USR(0):RETURN
300 POKE 1,27:X=USR(0):POKE 1,75:X=USR(0)
310 POKE 1,120:X=USR(0):POKE 1,0:X=USR(0):RETURN
392 DATA 0,1,7,1,15,7,3,15
393 DATA 0,128,224,128,240,224,192,240
394 DATA 3,3,3,7,31,63,63,0
395 DATA 192,192,192,224,248,252,252,0
396 DATA 0,1,15,7,3,15,7,3
397 DATA 0,128,240,224,192,240,224,192
398 DATA 3,3,3,7,31,63,63,0
399 DATA 192,192,192,224,248,252,252,0
400 DATA 0,0,13,13,15,7,7,7
401 DATA 0,0,176,176,240,224,224,224
402 DATA 7,7,7,7,15,31,31,0
403 DATA 224,224,224,224,240,248,248,0
404 DATA 0,0,1,3,7,3,15,3
405 DATA 0,0,128,192,224,192,240,192
406 DATA 3,3,3,7,15,31,31,0
407 DATA 192,192,192,224,240,248,248,0
408 DATA 0,0,0,3,15,63,57,3
409 DATA 0,0,192,240,248,252,252,252
410 DATA 7,15,15,7,15,31,31,0
411 DATA 248,240,240,224,240,248,248,0
412 DATA 0,0,0,0,3,7,7,3
413 DATA 0,0,0,0,192,224,224,192
414 DATA 15,3,3,7,15,31,31,0
415 DATA 240,192,192,224,240,248,248,0
416 DATA 85,169,87,161,79,167,83,175
417 DATA 85,138,229,138,245,234,197,242
```

100

```
418 DATA 83,171,83,167,95,191,63,170
419 DATA 197,202,213,234,249,252,253,170
420 DATA 85,161,79,167,83,175,71,163
421 DATA 85,130,245,234,197,242,229,202
422 DATA 83,171,83,167,95,191,63,170
423 DATA 213,202,197,226,249,252,253,170
424 DATA 85,170,77,173,79,167,71,167
425 DATA 85,170,181,178,245,234,229,234
426 DATA 71,167,71,167,79,159,95,170
427 DATA 229,234,229,234,245,250,249,170
428 DATA 85,170,85,171,87,163,79,163
429 DATA 85,42,149,202,229,202,245,202
430 DATA 83,163,83,167,79,159,95,170
431 DATA 213,202,213,234,245,250,249,170
432 DATA 85,170,84,163,79,191,57,131
433 DATA 85,42,197,242,249,252,253,252
434 DATA 71,175,79,167,79,159,95,170
435 DATA 249,250,245,226,245,250,249,170
436 DATA 85,170,85,168,83,167,87,163
437 DATA 85,170,85,10,197,234,229,202
438 DATA 79,163,83,167,79,159,95,170
439 DATA 245,202,197,226,241,250,249,170
READY
```

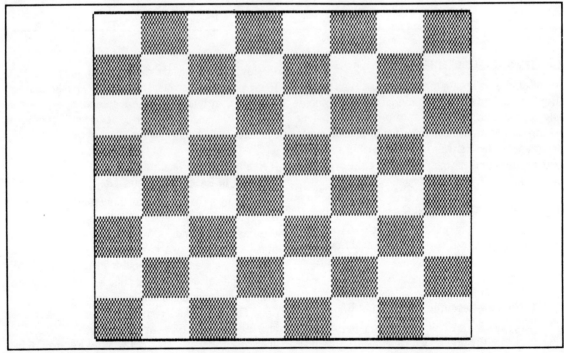

Fig. 6-2. A chessboard.

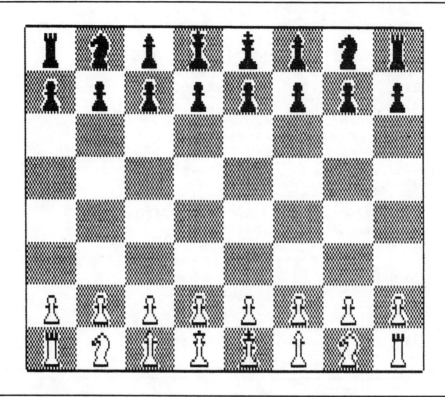

Fig. 6-3. A chessboard with chessmen.

MATHEMATICALLY DEFINED ART

Computers are mathematical tools and as such they can compute numbers at high speed. Computers can use their talents to draw pictures, provided that those pictures are defined mathematically. If a program can be written that will enable the computer to use numbers to draw images, the artist will have a new tool at his disposal.

We will now look at a few BASIC programs that display realistic and abstract art. By realistic, we mean resembling reality, the world as we see it. By abstract, we mean an exaggeration of reality, an unreality, if you will. Both have their proper place in art.

A Realistic Low-Resolution Program in BASIC

Program 8, the low-resolution perspective line plotter in Chapter 4, which showed a pyramid, a cube, and two diamonds, is an example of a realis-

tic low-resolution art program. It is considered low-resolution because we used asterisks instead of special graphic characters to show positions of points. Please refer back to it as an example of realistic low-resolution art.

A Realistic High-Resolution Program in BASIC—Program 19

Figures 6-4 to 6-6 are show figures produced by a realistic high-resolution art program. Although the images in Figures 6-5 and 6-6 are larger than that in 6-4, they are of slightly lower resolution. They also have an additional feature; they contain three types of shading: solid black, gray, and white. This is a trinary color scheme, not a simple binary one. The solid black represents the void of space, and the gray, the black areas of the ship. The white areas are the white area of the ship. Figure 6-6 is a longer version of Figure 6-5. It is 50% longer.

```
10 REM              HIGH RESOLUTION REALISTIC ART
20 REM              WRITTEN BY TIMOTHY J. O'MALLEY
30 REM              COPYRIGHT 1982, TAB BOOKS INC.
40 REM
50 PRINT CHR$(12)
60 GOSUB 3000:REM   BLANK GRAPHICS
70 GOSUB 2000:REM   PLACE GRAPHICS ON SCREEN
80 GOSUB 1000:REM   DEFINE GRAPHIC SET #1
90 GOSUB 1000:REM   DEFINE GRAPHIC SET #2
100 PRINT CHR$(12)::REM BLANK SCREEN (SOME CAN USE CLS)
110 GOSUB 4000:REM DEFINE TRINARY GRAPHICS
120 GOSUB 5000:REM READ DATA FOR IMAGE
190 END
200 DATA 88
210 DATA 24,0,1,3,7,7,15,14,30,112,252,246,143,248,0,0,31
220 DATA 0,0,0,0,128,192,32,160
230 DATA 104
240 DATA 24,31,56,32,32,33,33,97,97,43,48,0,0,255,0,0,0
250 DATA 208,24,8,228,252,66,66,66
260 DATA 96
270 DATA 32,0,0,0,1,1,1,3,3,97,225,225,225,225,225,225,225
280 DATA 0,0,0,255,0,0,0,0,66,66,66,253,66,66,66,66
290 DATA 96
300 DATA 32,3,7,7,11,11,19,35,68,241,241,241,241,241,241,241
    ,17
310 DATA 0,0,255,0,0,0,0,0,66,66,252,66,66,66,66,66
320 DATA 80
330 DATA 64,0,0,0,0,3,12,19,36,1,6,27,108,176,192,0,0
340 DATA 152,224,0,0,0,0,0,0,17,17,17,17,17,33,33,33
350 DATA 0,255,0,0,0,0,0,0,66,254,71,66,66,66,66,66
360 DATA 0,0,128,192,48,24,6,3,0,0,0,0,0,0,0,128
370 DATA 64
380 DATA 64,72,96,112,255,135,224,31,0,0,0,0,255,255,35,160,
    126
390 DATA 0,0,0,0,254,255,3,3,35,38,36,36,40,232,200,200
400 DATA 255,0,0,0,0,0,0,0,254,126,115,92,70,67,65,64
410 DATA 0,0,0,128,96,96,255,127,224,112,28,14,6,3,255,255
420 DATA 72
430 DATA 56,1,0,0,0,0,0,0,243,13,5,5,3,3,0,0
440 DATA 201,217,254,248,240,255,127,1,255,152,136,248,31
    ,247
450 DATA 248,255,216,87,49,24,247,224,192,128,28,12,199,54
460 DATA 142,102,30,0,3,30,224,0,0,0,0,0
470 DATA 128
500 DATA 49
510 DATA 23,1,3,6,15,12,24,17,112,252,174,115,143,1,0,252
```

```
520 DATA 0,0,0,0,128,128,192,64
530 DATA 104
540 DATA 24,54,38,32,32,63,32,96,96,171,115,0,216,255,32,32
550 DATA 32,96,32,32,32,224,32,48,48
560 DATA 99
570 DATA 29,1,1,1,3,3,96,224,224,255,224,224,224,224,32,32
    ,32
580 DATA 255,32,32,32,32,48,56,56,252,60,60,62,62
590 DATA 96
600 DATA 40,7,7,15,15,23,23,39,72,224,224,255,224,224,224
610 DATA 224,32,32,32,255,32,32,32,32,32,63,63,255,63,63
620 DATA 63,63,32,0,0,128,128,64,64,32,16
630 DATA 76
640 DATA 68,1,6,27,108,1,6,27,108,176,192,0,0,176,192
650 DATA 0,00,0,0,0,0,32,63,32,32,32,32,32,32,32,255,32,32
    ,32,32
660 DATA 32,32,32,224,32,32,32,32,32,32,108,27,6,1,0,0,0,0,0
    ,0
670 DATA 192,176,108,27,6,1,0,0,0,0,0,0,192,176
680 DATA 48
690 DATA 79,1,3,6,7,7,6,3,0,176,64,128,255,255,1,254,1,0,0,0
    ,255
700 DATA 255,255,64,255,0,0,1,254,254,254,2,130,127,192,0,0
    ,0,0
710 DATA 0,0,255,32,32,112,112,112,112,112,240,24,4,7,3,3,2
    ,2,0
720 DATA 0,0,255,255,255,0,15,0,0,0,255,255,252,19,252,108
    ,22,11
730 DATA 255,255,3,247
740 DATA 73
750 DATA 33,127,3,3,0,0,0,0,0,127,111,198,246,227,65,127,0
    ,255
760 DATA 119,115,115,254,252,255,32,247,182,30,120,56,16,240
770 DATA 0,240
780 DATA 183
1000 REM          DEFINE GRAPHICS
1010 A=-1025:M=0
1020 FOR J=1 TO 15:READ Z:N=0
1030 FOR K=1 TO Z:A=A+1:IF M<0 THEN READ N
1040 POKE A,N
1050 NEXT K:M=NOT(M):NEXT J
1060 RETURN
2000 REM          PLACE GRAPHICS ON SCREEN
2010 FOR Q=192 TO 1216 STEP 512
2020 FOR P=Q-3968 TO Q-3920 STEP 16
2030 L=127
```

```
2040 FOR J=P TO P+511 STEP 64
2050 FOR K=0 TO 15
2060 L=L+1
2070 POKE (J+K),L
2080 NEXT K,J,P,Q
2090 RETURN
3000 REM               BLANK GRAPHICS
3010 FOR J=-1024 TO -1
3020 POKE J,0
3030 NEXT J
3040 RETURN
4000 REM               DEFINE TRINARY GRAPHICS
4010 FOR J=-1024 TO -1:POKE J,0:NEXT J
4020 FOR R=1 TO 4:J=0:M=3^(R-1)
4030 V=0
4040 FOR K=1 TO M:N=J*8-1024:N1=N-(R>2)*4
4050 N2=N+3-(R>2)*4:IF V=0 THEN 4120
4060 IF V=1 THEN N3=160+(R/2=INT(R/2))*150
4070 IF V=2 THEN N3=240+(R/2=INT(R/2))*225
4080 Z=0:FOR P=N1 TO N2
4090 IFV=1 THEN POKEP,(PEEK(P)OR(N3/(1-Z))):Z=NOTZ:GOTO4110
4100 POKE P,(PEEK(P) OR N3)
4110 NEXT P
4120 J=J+1:NEXT K:V=V+1:IF V<3 AND J<81 THEN 4040
4130 IF V=3 AND J<81 THEN 4030
4140 NEXT R:RETURN
5000 REM               READ DATA FOR TRINARY IMAGE
5010 FOR J=1 TO 20:FOR K=1 TO 27
5020 READ XX:PRINT TAB(20);CHR$(XX);
5030 NEXT K:PRINT:NEXT J:RETURN
6000 REM               DATA FOR TRINARY IMAGE
6010 DATA 128,128,128,128,128,128,128,128,128,128,128
6020 DATA 164,168,165,137,128,128,128,128,128,128,128
6030 DATA 128,128,128,128,128
6040 DATA 128,128,128,128,128,128,128,128,128,128,194
6050 DATA 204,208,178,168,137,128,128,128,128,128,128
6060 DATA 128,128,128,128,128
6070 DATA 128,128,128,128,128,128,128,128,128,167,172
6080 DATA 172,199,208,168,165,128,128,128,128,128,128
6090 DATA 128,128,128,128,128
6100 DATA 128,128,128,128,128,128,128,128,158,180,199
6110 DATA 208,204,208,208,177,128,128,128,128,128,128
6120 DATA 128,128,128,128,128
6130 DATA 128,128,128,128,128,128,128,128,195,177,204
6140 DATA 204,204,177,208,178,138,128,128,128,128,128
6150 DATA 128,128,128,128,128
```

```
6160 DATA 128,128,128,128,128,128,128,158,208,178,208
6170 DATA 208,208,178,208,178,138,128,128,128,128,128
6180 DATA 128,128,128,128,128
6190 DATA 128,128,128,128,128,128,128,158,172,169,172
6200 DATA 172,172,169,208,178,168,128,128,128,128,128
6210 DATA 128,128,128,128,128
6220 DATA 128,128,128,128,128,128,128,158,208,178,208
6230 DATA 208,208,178,208,178,168,137,128,128,128,128
6240 DATA 128,128,128,128,128
6250 DATA 128,128,128,128,128,128,128,158,208,178,208
6260 DATA 208,208,178,208,168,168,138,128,128,128,128
6270 DATA 128,128,128,128,128
6280 DATA 128,128,128,128,128,128,128,158,204,177,204
6290 DATA 204,204,177,208,168,168,195,137
6300 DATA 128,128,128,128,128,128,128,128
6310 DATA 128,128,128,128,128,128,128,158,208,178,208
6320 DATA 208,208,178,208,168,168,171,204,137,128,128
6330 DATA 128,128,128,128,128
6340 DATA 128,128,128,128,128,128,128,167,172,169,172
6350 DATA 172,172,169,208,198,208,208,204,169,195,164
6360 DATA 128,128,128,128,128
6370 DATA 128,128,128,128,128,155,194,177,208,178,208
6380 DATA 208,208,178,208,198,208,208,208,208,205,180
6390 DATA 195,164,137,128,128
6400 DATA 128,128,128,155,167,207,208,178,208,178,208
6410 DATA 208,208,178,208,198,208,208,208,208,208,208
6420 DATA 208,204,196,137,128
6430 DATA 128,128,164,204,208,208,208,169,177,168,204
6440 DATA 204,204,204,168,180,208,208,208,208,208,172
6450 DATA 172,172,169,169,128
6460 DATA 128,167,207,208,208,172,172,195,207,178,208
6470 DATA 208,208,208,178,205,169,168,168,168,168,177
6480 DATA 204,204,168,168,129
6490 DATA 158,195,204,204,204,168,204,181,172,168,172
6500 DATA 172,172,172,178,208,168,172,172,172,142,132
6510 DATA 132,132,128,128,128
6520 DATA 128,132,132,132,168,181,196,207,169,168,172
6530 DATA 205,172,204,177,168,168,142,128,128,128,128
6540 DATA 128,128,128,128,128
6550 DATA 128,128,128,128,168,172,132,132,131,171,172
6560 DATA 172,141,132,129,128,128,128,128,128,128,128
6570 DATA 128,128,128,128,128
6580 DATA 128,128,128,128,128,128,128,128,128,132,132
6590 DATA 132,129,128,128,128,128,128,128,128,128
6600 DATA 128,128,128,128,128
READY
```

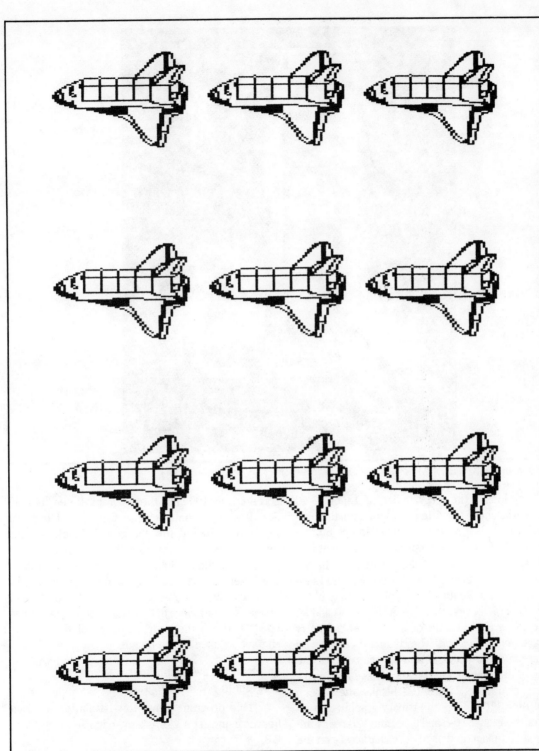

Fig. 6-4. Side view of space shuttles created using the handmade method.

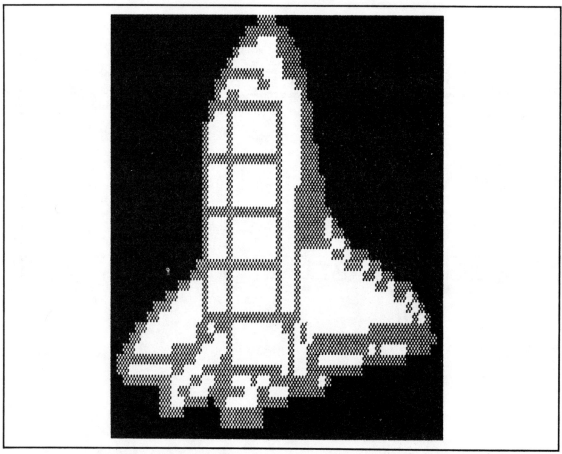

Fig. 6-5. A shortened trinary-colored space shuttle.

Let's look at the program listing. Lines 10-40 are remarks about the title and credits for the program. After a clear screen command in line 50, the computer goes to the subroutine that starts at line 3000. This sets all the user-defined graphic characters to zero, or blank. Line 70 goes to the subroutine at line 2000 which pokes those blank graphic characters on the screen. Lines 80 and 90 define the graphic character set that is currently displayed on the screen. The characters change on the screen as the data statements are read for the points of the graphic characters. These are binary graphic characters. Line 100 blanks the screen again. Line 110 defines the trinary graphic characters for the Figures 6-5 and 6-6. Line 120 reads the data for the image and prints the characters on the screen. Line 190 ends the program. Lines 200-780 are data statements for the first set of images. Lines 1000-1060 define the graphic characters for the binary images. Lines 2000-2090 place them on the screen. Lines 3000-3040 blank those graphic characters. Lines 4000-4140 define the trinary graphics. Lines 5000-5030 read data for the trinary image. The numbers in the data statements in lines 6000-6600 are the code numbers of the graphic characters used in the image.

An Abstract Low-Resolution Program in BASIC—Program 20

This program prints low-resolution abstract figures using asterisks as shown in Figures 6-7 and 6-8.

108

Fig. 6-6. A trinary-colored space shuttle.

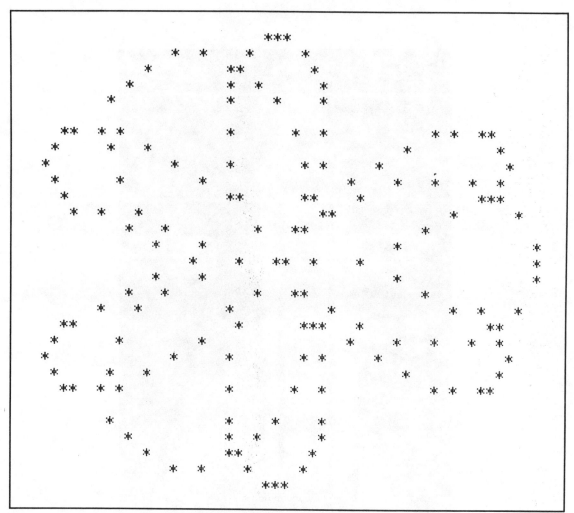

Fig. 6-7. Two overlapping polar coordinate figures.

```
10 REM              ABSTRACT, LOW-RESOLUTION ART
20 REM              WRITTEN BY TIMOTHY J. O'MALLEY
30 REM              COPYRIGHT 1982, TAB BOOKS INC.
40 REM
45 GOSUB 500:REM     DISPLAY AND QUESTION
50 DIM X(500),Y(500):REM RESERVE SPACE FOR UP TO 500 POINTS
60 K=0:REM          SET POINT COUNTER TO ZERO
70 READ N:REM       NUMBER OF DIFFERENT FIGURES PLOTTED
80 PRINT CHR$(12);:FOR H=1 TO N
90 READ M,R,P,S,D:REM MAGNIFICATION,ROTATIONS,POINTS,SIZING
   ,DISP
100 C=6.28319*R:REM    TOTAL ROTATION IN RADIANS
```

```
110 FOR J=C/P TO C STEP C/P
120 L=ABS(SIN(0.5*M*J)):REM DISTANCE OF POINT FROM ORIGIN
130 K=K+1:REM            INCREMENT COUNTER
140 X(K)=L*28*COS(J+D):REM ORIGINAL HORIZONTAL POSITION
150 Y(K)=L*14*SIN(J+D):REM ORIGINAL VERTICAL POSITION
160 IF S=1 THEN X(K)=X(K)*J/C:Y(K)=Y(K)*J/C
170 IF S=-1 THEN X(K)=X(K)*(1-J/C):Y(K)=Y(K)*(1-J/C)
180 X(K)=INT(X(K)+28.5)
190 Y(K)=INT(Y(K)+14.5)
200 NEXT J,H
210 FOR J=1 TO K-1
220 FOR H=J+1 TO K
230 IF Y(J)>Y(H) THEN 280
240 IF Y(J)<Y(H) THEN 260
250 IF X(J)<=X(H) THEN 280
260 A=X(J):X(J)=X(H):X(H)=A
270 B=Y(J):Y(J)=Y(H):Y(H)=B
280 NEXT H,J
290 J=1:GOSUB 390
300 FOR J=2 TO K
310 IF Y(J-1)>Y(J) THEN GOSUB 350
320 IF X(J)<>X(J-1) AND Y(J)<=Y(J-1) THEN GOSUB 390
330 NEXT J
340 END
350 FOR H=Y(J) TO Y(J-1)-1
360 PRINT
370 NEXT H
380 RETURN
390 PRINT TAB(X(J));"*";
400 RETURN
410 DATA 3:REM   N
420 DATA 6,1,120,0,0
430 DATA 3,1,60,0,1.0472
440 DATA 0.01,1,50,0,0
500 REM                 DISPLAY AND QUESTION
510 PRINT CHR$(12);
520 PRINT:PRINT:PRINT:PRINT
530 PRINT TAB(15);
540 PRINT"ABSTRACT, LOW-RESOLUTION ART"
550 PRINT TAB(14);
560 PRINT "WRITTEN BY TIMOTHY J. O'MALLEY"
570 PRINT TAB(14);
580 PRINT "COPYRIGHT 1982, TAB BOOKS INC."
590 PRINT:PRINT:PRINT
600 INPUT "DO YOU WANT INSTRUCTIONS (YES OR NO)";AN$
610 IF AN$="NO" THEN RETURN
```

```
620 PRINT
630 PRINT:PRINT
640 PRINT "     This program prints out polar coordinate
    plots."
650 PRINT "There are several parameters: N, which is the
    number"
660 PRINT "of different figures plotted together;M,which is"
670 PRINT "a multiplication factor for the radians of the"
680 PRINT "rotation; R, which is the number of complete "
690 PRINT "rotations; P, which is the number of points in"
700 PRINT "each figure; S,which is for growing or shrinking"
710 PRINT "figures as they rotate about the origin; and D, "
720 PRINT "which is the displacement, in radians, of the"
730 PRINT "figure about the origin when plotted."
740 PRINT:PRINT:PRINT
750 INPUT "When finished reading, press RETURN. OK";AN$
760 RETURN
READY
```

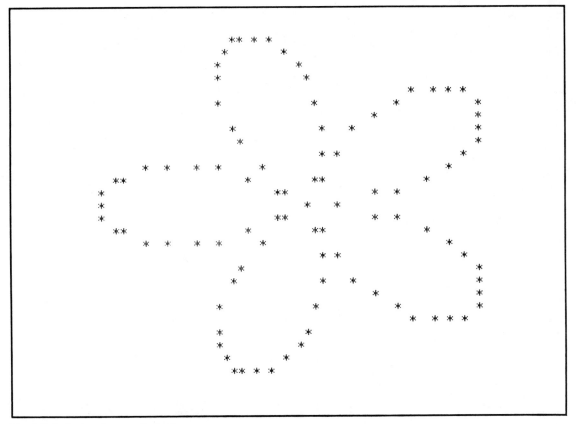

Fig. 6-8. A single polar coordinate figure.

Let's look at the program. Lines 10-40 give the title and credits in remark statements. Line 45 is a subroutine call to line 500. Line 50 is a dimension statement which reserves memory space to hold the coordinates for up to 500 points. Line 60 sets the point counter to zero. Line 70 reads the number of different figures to be plotted on the same graph. Lines 80-200 contain two nested loops which read in the data and compute the coordinates of the points. The loops also sort the points so that they can be printed from top to bottom, and from left to

short program that we will examine now. These figures resemble moire patterns but were produced in a different way. The program is very simple.

Lines 10-40 give the title and credits. Line 50 calls a subroutine at line 300 which sets up a machine-language subroutine to pass numbers to the printer. Line 60 calls the main program at line 100. Line 70 ends the program. We can change this program to a low-resolution program that does not use a machine-language subroutine, but let's look at the main program a bit first.

```
10 REM                MOIRE PATTERNS
20 REM        WRITTEN BY TIMOTHY J. O'MALLEY
30 REM         COPYRIGHT 1982, TAB BOOKS INC.
40 REM
50 GOSUB 300:REM INITIALIZE PROGRAM
60 GOSUB 100:REM MAIN PROGRAM
70 END
100 REM                MAIN PROGRAM
105 FOR P=0.1 TO 1.0 STEP 0.1
110 FOR Y=-240 TO 240:Y2=Y*Y
120 FOR X=-240 TO 239:IF X/80=INT(X/80) THEN GOSUB 400
130 R=INT((1E7*(Y2+X*X))^P)
140 IF R/2-INT(R/2) THEN POKE 1,N1:XX=USR(0):GOTO 170
160 POKE 1,0:XX=USR(0)
170 NEXT X:POKE 1,13:XX=USR(0):NEXT Y:POKE 1,12:XX=USR(0)
180 NEXT P:END
300 REM                INITIALIZE PROGRAM
310 N1=2:REM PIN POSITION USED FOR PRINTING
320 POKE 260,0:POKE 261,0:POKE 0,62:POKE 1,27
330 POKE 2,205:POKE 3,12:POKE 4,224:POKE 5,201
340 XX=USR(0):POKE 1,65:XX=USR(0):POKE 1,1:XX=USR(0)
350 RETURN
400 POKE 1,27:XX=USR(0):POKE 1,75:XX=USR(0)
410 POKE 1,80:XX=USR(0):POKE 1,0:XX=USR(0):RETURN
READY
```

right. Lines 290-400 include the lines that print out the final figures. The data statements in lines 410-440 contain information concerning what to plot. Lines 500-760 give the instructions.

An Abstract High-Resolution
Program in BASIC—Program 21

Figures 6-9 to 6-17 were all made by the same

In lines 100-180 of the main program, we have three loops that are nested. The first loop, containing the variable P, is for the power of a number in the program. The Y and X loops are for the X and Y coordinates. Line 130 computes R, which is the integer of 1E7 times X squared plus Y squared to the power of P. Line 140 says that if R is an even number, print a dot; line 160 says otherwise, print a

Fig. 6-9. Moire pattern at P=0.1.

Fig. 6-10. Moire pattern at P=0.2.

Fig. 6-11. Moire pattern at P=0.3.

Fig. 6-12. Moire pattern at P=0.4.

117

Fig. 6-13. Moire pattern at P=0.5.

Fig. 6-14. Moire pattern at P=0.6.

119

Fig. 6-15. Moire pattern at P=0.7.

Fig. 6-16. Moire pattern at P=0.8.

Fig. 6-17. Moire pattern at P=0.9.

blank dot. It's that simple! You could change the program so that it would print an asterisk if R was even and a space if R was odd. Then you would not need to use high-resolution graphics or machine-language subroutines to pass numbers to the printer. In all of these figures the dark points are where even numbers are found, and the light points are where odd numbers are found.

Another Abstract
High-Resolution Art Program—Program 22

Figure 6-18 shows the result of rotating and shrinking a triangle. This figure was made by displaying user-defined graphic characters on the screen and then doing a screen dump to place the figure onto paper. The triangle is turning clockwise as it is shrinking. Let's briefly look at the program.

```
10 REM             HIGH RESOLUTION ABSTRACT ART
20 REM             WRITTEN BY TIMOTHY J. O'MALLEY
30 REM             COPYRIGHT 1982, TAB BOOKS INC.
40 REM
50 GOSUB 300:REM     INITIALIZE VARIABLES
80 GOSUB 800:REM     TRANSLATE X,Y,Z TO H,V
90 GOSUB 500:REM     BLANK GRAPHICS
100 GOSUB 1200:REM   DRAW LINES CONNECTING POINTS
110 GOSUB 1600:REM DUMP GRAPHICS TO PRINTER
290 END
300 REM             INITIALIZE VARIABLES
305 IP=72
307 IA=120
310 DIM I(IA),X(IP),Y(IP),Z(IP),R(3),V(IP),H(IP)
320 FOR J=1 TO IP STEP 3
325 M=EXP((300-J)/100)
326 O=J/15
330 X(J)=M*SIN(O)
331 Y(J)=0
332 Z(J)=M*COS(O)
334 X(J+1)=M*SIN(2.0944+O)
335 Y(J+1)=0
336 Z(J+1)=M*COS(2.0944+O)
337 X(J+2)=M*SIN(4.1888+O)
338 Y(J+2)=0
339 Z(J+2)=M*COS(4.1888+O)
340 NEXT J
350 I1=1:I2=2:I3=3
380 FOR J=1 TO IA STEP 5
381 I(J)=I1
382 I(J+1)=I2
383 I(J+2)=I3
384 I(J+3)=I1
385 I(J+4)=0
386 I1=I1+3:I2=I2+3:I3=I3+3
400 NEXT J
420 R(1)=18:R(2)=24:R(3)=14
```

```
430 X(0)=10:Y(0)=-50:Z(0)=7
440 F=.1:G=100
450 S=1:T=IP
460 B$="Z"
470 W=15.875:U=7.875:REM WIDTH AND HEIGHT OF SCREEN
480 E=0.4:REM ROTATION INCREMENT
490 RETURN
500 REM                  BLANK GRAPHICS
510 PRINT CHR$(12);:REM BLANK SCREEN
520 POKE -3968,32:REM ERASE CURSOR FROM SCREEN
530 FOR J=-1024 TO -1
540 POKE J,0
550 NEXT J
560 FOR J=0 TO 127:REM PLACE GRAPHICS ON SCREEN
570 POKE (J-3240+48*INT(J/16)),(J+128)
580 NEXT J
590 RETURN
600 REM                  ROTATE POINTS ABOUT AXIS
610 FOR J=S TO T
620 IF B$="Z" THEN A1=X(J):A2=R(1):A3=Y(J):A4=R(2)
630 IF B$="Y" THEN A1=X(J):A2=R(1):A3=Z(J):A4=R(3)
640 IF B$="X" THEN A1=Y(J):A2=R(2):A3=Z(J):A4=R(3)
650 P1=A1-A2:P2=A3-A4
660 L=SQR(P1*P1+P2*P2)
670 IF P2=0 THEN A5=0-(P1<0)*3.141593
680 IF P1=0 THEN A5=SGN(P2)*1.570796
690 IF P2<>0 AND P1<>0 THEN A5=ATN(P2/P1)-(P1<0)*3.141593
700 A5=A5+E
710 IF B$="Z" THEN X(J)=L*COS(A5)+R(1):Y(J)=L*SIN(A5)+R(2)
720 IF B$="Y" THEN X(J)=L*COS(A5)+R(1):Z(J)=L*SIN(A5)+R(3)
730 IF B$="X" THEN Y(J)=L*COS(A5)+R(2):Z(J)=L*SIN(A5)+R(3)
740 NEXT J
750 RETURN
800 REM                  TRANSLATE X,Y,Z TO H,V
810 FOR J=1 TO IP
820 DY=Y(J)-Y(0):IF DY<=0 THEN PRINT "DECREASE Y(0)":STOP
830 DX=X(J)-X(0)
840 DZ=Z(J)-Z(0)
850 V(J)=G*ATN(F*DZ/DY):REM VERTICAL SCREEN POSITION
860 H(J)=G*ATN(F*DX/DY):REM HORIZONTAL SCREEN POSITION
870 NEXT J
880 MINV=V(1):MAXV=V(1)
890 MINH=H(1):MAXH=H(1)
900 FOR J=1 TO IP
910 IF V(J)<MINV THEN MINV=V(J)
920 IF V(J)>MAXV THEN MAXV=V(J)
```

```
930 IF H(J)<MINH THEN MINH=H(J)
940 IF H(J)>MAXH THEN MAXH=H(J)
950 NEXT J
960 DH=MAXH-MINH
970 DV=MAXV-MINV
980 FOR J=1 TO IP
990 H(J)=(H(J)-MINH)/DH*W
1000 V(J)=(V(J)-MINV)/DV*U
1110 NEXT J
1120 RETURN
1200 REM                DRAW LINES CONNECTING POINTS
1210 FOR J=1 TO IA-1
1220 IF I(J)=0 OR I(J+1)=0 THEN 1340
1230 HH=H(I(J+1))-H(I(J))
1240 VV=V(I(J+1))-V(I(J))
1250 SN=SGN(HH)
1260 IF SN=0 THEN 1360
1270 M=VV/HH
1280 B=V(I(J))-M*H(I(J))
1290 SP=SQR(VV*VV+HH*HH)
1300 FOR K=H(I(J)) TO H(I(J+1)) STEP 0.125*HH/SP
1310 P=M*K+B
1320 GOSUB 1500
1330 NEXT K
1340 NEXT J
1350 RETURN
1360 REM                SLOPE EQUALS INFINITY
1370 K=H(I(J))
1380 IF SGN(VV)=0 THEN P=H(I(J)):GOSUB 1500:GOTO 1340
1390 FOR P=V(I(J)) TO V(I(J+1)) STEP 0.125*SGN(VV)
1400 GOSUB 1500
1410 NEXT P
1420 GOTO 1340
1430 GOTO 1310
1500 REM                PLOTTING SUBOUTINE
1510 IF P>U OR P<0 OR K>W OR K<0 THEN RETURN
1520 Q=INT(K)*8-121-128*INT(P)-INT(8*(P-INT(P)))
1530 POKE Q,(PEEK(Q) OR 2^(7-INT(8*(K-INT(K)))))
1540 RETURN
1600 REM        DUMP GRAPHICS TO PRINTER
1610 POKE 260,0:POKE 261,0:POKE 0,62:POKE 1,27
1620 POKE 2,205:POKE 3,12:POKE 4,224:POKE 5,201
1630 X=USR(0):POKE 1,65:X=USR(0):POKE 1,2:X=USR(0)
1640 FOR M=0 TO 63:C1=120*INT(M/8)-1024+M
1650 FOR P=0 TO 1:C2=C1+64*P:POKE 1,27:X=USR(0)
1660 POKE 1,75:X=USR(0):POKE 1,64:X=USR(0):POKE 1,0
```

```
1670 X=USR(0):FOR J=0 TO 7:C3=PEEK(C2+8*J)
1680 FOR N=7 TO 0 STEP -1
1690 POKE 1,3*SGN(2^N AND C3)
1700 X=USR(0):NEXT N,J,P:POKE 1,13:X=USR(0)
1710 NEXT M:POKE 1,12:X=USR(0):RETURN
READY
```

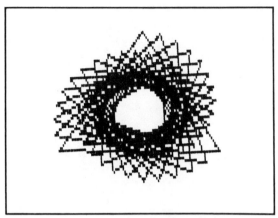

Fig. 6-18. Abstract art, the rotating shrinking triangle.

as the perspective line-plotting programs did. Lines 500-590 blank the graphic characters and then place them correctly on the screen. Lines 1200-1420 draw lines connecting the vertices for the sides of the triangle. Lines 1600-1710 are a screen-dump routine which sends the image to the printer.

You might change some of these lines to produce a low-resolution program. Use the low-resolution perspective line plotter in Chapter 4 as a guide.

A Final High-Resolution Abstract Art Program—Program 23

The images in Fig. 6-19 are the results of running the next program. These two images are oscillating lines that spiral clockwise to the center of the figures. Notice that in the lower image the lines on the right half have turned white instead of black and the lower part of the image has half of the vertical columns of lines missing.

First the program sets up the arrays and variables using the subroutine in lines 300-490. It computes the coordinates of the three vertices which the program will later rotate about an axis. The subroutine in lines 800-1120 translates these coordinates into a horizontal and vertical position, just

```
10  REM               HIGH RESOLUTION ABSTRACT ART
20  REM               WRITTEN BY TIMOTHY J. O'MALLEY
30  REM               COPYRIGHT 1982, TAB BOOKS INC.
40  REM
50  GOSUB 300:REM      INITIALIZE VARIABLES
80  GOSUB 800:REM      TRANSLATE X,Y,Z TO H,V
90  GOSUB 500:REM      BLANK GRAPHICS
100 GOSUB 1200:REM    DRAW LINES CONNECTING POINTS
110 GOSUB 1600:REM     DUMP GRAPHICS TO PRINTER
120 GOSUB 2000:REM      ALTER GRAPHICS BY SHADING
130 GOSUB 1600:PRINT CHR$(12)
140 END
300 REM                INITIALIZE VARIABLES
305 IP=300
307 IA=IP
310 DIM I(IA),X(IP),Y(IP),Z(IP),R(3),V(IP),H(IP)
```

```
320 FOR J=1 TO IP STEP 2
325 M=EXP((300-J)/100)
326 O=J/15
330 X(J)=M*SIN(O)
331 Y(J)=0
332 Z(J)=M*COS(O)
334 X(J+1)=(M*2)*SIN(O)
335 Y(J+1)=0
336 Z(J+1)=(M*2)*COS(O)
340 NEXT J
350 I1=1:I2=2:I3=3
380 FOR J=1 TO IP
381 I(J)=J
382 NEXT J
420 R(1)=18:R(2)=24:R(3)=14
430 X(0)=10:Y(0)=-50:Z(0)=7
440 F=.1:G=100
450 S=1:T=IP
460 B$="Z"
470 W=15.875:U=7.875:REM WIDTH AND HEIGHT OF SCREEN
480 E=0.4:REM ROTATION INCREMENT
490 RETURN
500 REM                    BLANK GRAPHICS
510 PRINT CHR$(12);:REM BLANK SCREEN
520 POKE -3968,32:REM ERASE CURSOR FROM SCREEN
530 FOR J=-1024 TO -1
540 POKE J,0
550 NEXT J
560 FOR J=0 TO 127:REM PLACE GRAPHICS ON SCREEN
570 POKE (J-3240+48*INT(J/16)),(J+128)
580 NEXT J
590 RETURN
600 REM                    ROTATE POINTS ABOUT AXIS
610 FOR J=S TO T
620 IF B$="Z" THEN A1=X(J):A2=R(1):A3=Y(J):A4=R(2)
630 IF B$="Y" THEN A1=X(J):A2=R(1):A3=Z(J):A4=R(3)
640 IF B$="X" THEN A1=Y(J):A2=R(2):A3=Z(J):A4=R(3)
650 P1=A1-A2:P2=A3-A4
660 L=SQR(P1*P1+P2*P2)
670 IF P2=0 THEN A5=0-(P1<0)*3.141593
680 IF P1=0 THEN A5=SGN(P2)*1.570796
690 IF P2<>0 AND P1<>0 THEN A5=ATN(P2/P1)-(P1<0)*3.141593
700 A5=A5+E
710 IF B$="Z" THEN X(J)=L*COS(A5)+R(1):Y(J)=L*SIN(A5)+R(2)
720 IF B$="Y" THEN X(J)=L*COS(A5)+R(1):Z(J)=L*SIN(A5)+R(3)
730 IF B$="X" THEN Y(J)=L*COS(A5)+R(2):Z(J)=L*SIN(A5)+R(3)
```

```
740 NEXT J
750 RETURN
800 REM                    TRANSLATE X,Y,Z TO H,V
810 FOR J=1 TO IP
820 DY=Y(J)-Y(0):IF DY<=0 THEN PRINT "DECREASE Y(0)":STOP
830 DX=X(J)-X(0)
840 DZ=Z(J)-Z(0)
850 V(J)=G*ATN(F*DZ/DY):REM VERTICAL SCREEN POSITION
860 H(J)=G*ATN(F*DX/DY):REM HORIZONTAL SCREEN POSITION
870 NEXT J
880 MINV=V(1):MAXV=V(1)
890 MINH=H(1):MAXH=H(1)
900 FOR J=1 TO IP
910 IF V(J)<MINV THEN MINV=V(J)
920 IF V(J)>MAXV THEN MAXV=V(J)
930 IF H(J)<MINH THEN MINH=H(J)
940 IF H(J)>MAXH THEN MAXH=H(J)
950 NEXT J
960 DH=MAXH-MINH
970 DV=MAXV-MINV
980 FOR J=1 TO IP
990 H(J)=(H(J)-MINH)/DH*W
1000 V(J)=(V(J)-MINV)/DV*U
1110 NEXT J
1120 RETURN
1200 REM                    DRAW LINES CONNECTING POINTS
1210 FOR J=1 TO IA-1
1220 IF I(J)=0 OR I(J+1)=0 THEN 1340
1230 HH=H(I(J+1))-H(I(J))
1240 VV=V(I(J+1))-V(I(J))
1250 SN=SGN(HH)
1260 IF SN=0 THEN 1360
1270 M=VV/HH
1280 B=V(I(J))-M*H(I(J))
1290 SP=SQR(VV*VV+HH*HH)
1300 FOR K=H(I(J)) TO H(I(J+1)) STEP 0.125*HH/SP
1310 P=M*K+B
1320 GOSUB 1500
1330 NEXT K
1340 NEXT J
1350 RETURN
1360 REM                    SLOPE EQUALS INFINITY
1370 K=H(I(J))
1380 IF SGN(VV)=0 THEN P=H(I(J)):GOSUB 1500:GOTO 1340
1390 FOR P=V(I(J)) TO V(I(J+1)) STEP 0.125*SGN(VV)
1400 GOSUB 1500
```

```
1410 NEXT P
1420 GOTO 1340
1430 GOTO 1310
1500 REM                PLOTTING SUBOUTINE
1510 IF P>U OR P<0 OR K>W OR K<0 THEN RETURN
1520 Q=INT(K)*8-121-128*INT(P)-INT(8*(P-INT(P)))
1530 POKE Q,(PEEK(Q) OR 2^(7-INT(8*(K-INT(K)))))
1540 RETURN
1600 REM           DUMP GRAPHICS TO PRINTER
1610 POKE 260,0:POKE 261,0:POKE 0,62:POKE 1,27
1620 POKE 2,205:POKE 3,12:POKE 4,224:POKE 5,201
1630 X=USR(0):POKE 1,65:X=USR(0):POKE 1,2:X=USR(0)
1640 FOR M=0 TO 63:C1=120*INT(M/8)-1024+M
1650 FOR P=0 TO 1:C2=C1+64*P:POKE 1,27:X=USR(0)
1660 POKE 1,75:X=USR(0):POKE 1,64:X=USR(0):POKE 1,0
1670 X=USR(0):FOR J=0 TO 7:C3=PEEK(C2+8*J)
1680 FOR N=7 TO 0 STEP -1
1690 POKE 1,3*SGN(2^N AND C3)
1700 X=USR(0):NEXT N,J,P:POKE 1,13:X=USR(0):NEXT M
1710 FOR J=1 TO 20:X=USR(0):NEXT J:RETURN
2000 FOR I=-960 TO -1 STEP 128
2010 FOR J=I TO I+63
2020 POKE J,(255-PEEK(J))
2030 NEXT J,I
2050 FOR J=-512 TO -1
2060 POKE J,(85 AND PEEK(J))
2070 NEXT J
2080 RETURN
READY
```

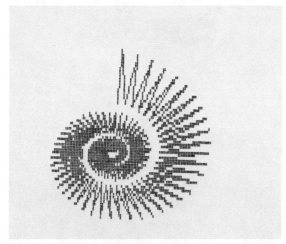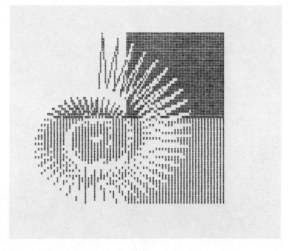

Fig. 6-19. Abstract art, spiralling lines.

We present the program listing but we will not look into it. What we did was simply to compute the positions of various points and connect lines between consecutive points. The final figures were displayed on the video screen and then dumped to the printer as in the last program. Again, you can change the program to suit your computer. With that, let's go on to animated graphics.

Chapter 7

Animated Graphics

Animated graphics are an interesting area of computer graphics. Unfortunately, many personal computers simply do not have the speed to handle animated graphics. Unless the graphics are simple, everything appears as if it is in slow motion. To solve that problem, programs are written in machine-language or at least use machine-language extensively. This change can speed up the apparent motion by the factor of 10.

TYPES OF ANIMATED GRAPHICS

Let's discuss a few types of animated graphics that are around today. One type is the video game, found in both arcades and home entertainment centers. Another type is the computer game that you load into your computer from tape or disk. Other types of animated graphics include models or simulations that are programmed into the computer but are not games.

Arcade-Type Video Games

The video game machines and the video computers generally contain only one program. That program is loaded as Read Only Memory and can not be changed, except by changing the ROM cartridge. The users of these games never see the programming. The programming is in binary or machine-language.

Programmable Games

Programmable games for the personal computer are of two types as we mentioned before: those in BASIC; and those in machine-language. Games in BASIC are likely to be understood by more programmers but may be slow. You may have to wait for a question mark prompt to appear before you can enter a response, although some versions of BASIC contain an INKEY$ function which allows the entry of characters without the display of a prompt. Other versions of BASIC would have to use a machine-language subroutine that would search to see if a key was pressed during a period of time. BASIC is really not intended to be the language for animated graphics.

Real-time simulations are better if they are written in machine-language. In real-time simulations, your responses are rapidly interpreted and the graphics reflect your action. Unlike BASIC, machine-language can look for your response and if it doesn't find one, it can still continue with the program.

Models and Simulations

Animated graphics can be used to model how something in the real world might act. Suppose you wanted to know how two galaxies would react if they were to collide. If you knew the forces in-

volved, you could make a simulation of the collision. In reality the process would take eons to occur, but with a computer model, you could see the results in seconds or minutes. This is an ideal example of the use of animated graphics for purposes other than entertainment.

ANIMATED GRAPHICS IN BASIC

Program 24 uses the poke function to place user-defined graphics on the screen. The image is supposed to represent a walking figure whose legs and arms move.

```
10 REM              ANIMATED GRAPHICS
20 REM         WRITTEN BY TIMOTHY J. O'MALLEY
30 REM           COPYRIGHT 1982, TAB BOOKS INC.
40 PRINT CHR$(12):REM CLEAR SCREEN (SOME CAN USE CLS)
50 DIM A(10,32)
60 FOR J=1 TO 10:FOR K=1 TO 32
70 READ A(J,K):NEXT K,J
80 POKE -3040,192:POKE -3039,193
90 POKE -2976,194:POKE -2975,195
100 FOR J=1 TO 10:FOR K=1 TO 32
110 POKE K-513,A(J,K)
120 NEXT K,J
130 GOTO 100
200 DATA 0,0,0,1,1,3,3,7,0,0,0,128,128,192,192,224
210 DATA 11,19,34,4,8,16,32,192,208,200,68,32,16,8,4,4
220 DATA 0,0,0,1,1,3,3,7,0,0,0,128,128,192,192,224
230 DATA 11,19,18,4,8,16,32,96,208,200,72,32,32,24,4,4
240 DATA 0,0,0,1,1,3,3,7,0,0,0,128,128,192,192,224
250 DATA 11,11,18,4,4,8,16,48,208,208,72,64,64,56,6,2
260 DATA 0,0,0,1,1,3,3,7,0,0,0,128,128,192,192,224
270 DATA 7,11,9,10,2,4,4,24,224,208,80,80,64,48,15,2
280 DATA 0,0,0,1,1,3,3,3,0,0,0,128,128,192,192,192
290 DATA 7,7,7,3,2,2,4,12,224,224,224,192,128,96,12,4
300 DATA 0,0,0,1,1,3,3,3,0,0,0,128,128,192,192,192
310 DATA 3,3,3,3,3,1,1,3,192,192,192,128,0,128,112,16
320 DATA 0,0,0,1,1,3,3,3,0,0,0,128,128,192,192,192
330 DATA 7,7,6,2,4,3,0,0,224,224,160,128,128,64,192,192
340 DATA 0,0,0,1,1,3,3,7,0,0,0,128,128,192,192,224
350 DATA 7,11,10,10,4,6,1,1,224,208,80,80,64,32,144,24
360 DATA 0,0,0,1,1,3,3,7,0,0,0,128,128,192,192,224
370 DATA 11,11,18,4,8,4,6,4,208,208,72,32,16,16,8,24
380 DATA 0,0,0,1,1,3,3,7,0,0,0,128,128,192,192,224
```

```
390 DATA 11,19,18,4,4,8,8,24,144,136,72,32,16,12,4,12
READY
```

Let's look at the program. The data contained in the lines 200-390 are numbers representing the bits of the image. The numbers range from 0 to 255 for the 8-bit numbers. To make the figure appear to walk, successive graphic characters are poked onto the screen and the old ones are erased. Thus the images change and motion is accomplished.

UTILIZING MOTION IN ANIMATION

Animated graphics use motion. Motion can give the illusion of depth to an image. Motion can be in more than one direction. A simple rotation of a figure could be considered motion in one direction. A baseball, as it is projected through the air, could illustrate motion in two directions since the vertical location and the horizontal location both change independently with time. A molecule has at least three types of motion: it has thermal vibration, rotation of one or more groups, and Brownian motion in whatever media it is in.

Motion in One Direction

We have seen motion in one direction in our molecular rotation model. Although that program was slow, it displayed the principle of motion in one direction. On the screen or on paper the image changes along one dimension. The stretching of a rubber band might be another example of motion in one direction. The length changes with time.

Motion in Two Directions

Motion in two direction includes the ballistic motion of a projectile through the air. If the projectile is spinning, it might be displaying motion in more than two directions. Another example is a Lissajous pattern made by a moving dot. The dot traces out points on the screen like an oscilloscope. The orbit of an object about another object is another example of motion in two directions.

Motion in Three Directions

In addition to rotating projectiles, examples of objects that have motion in three directions include the path of a fly buzzing through the air, the cycloid motion of a tire, the motion of the moon around the earth while both revolve around the sun. The list is endless.

ACCOMPLISHING MOTION

There are several techniques that you can use to simulate motion. You can print points and then erase them. If you are using a BASIC language that has the poke function, you can use that function to place points on the screen and then place blank points on the screen to erase them. If you are using machine-language subroutines and the USR function, you can change the image rapidly to give the illusion of motion. There are also other ways.

Printing and Erasing

If you write a program that has a print statement such as **PRINT "*";** followed by a statement like **PRINT CHR$(8);** the program will print an asterisk and then erase it. If you direct computer control back to the first statement, it will enter an endless loop and the result will be a blinking asterisk. Unfortunately, some computers insert a carriage return after every 64 or 80 characters printed. By using control characters that tab the cursor to the proper position on the screen, without erasing points in the process, and then erasing the character in question, you can print and erase points to accomplish motion in BASIC. This process is slow. As we said before, BASIC is really not the language for animated graphics.

Using the Poke Function

The speed of printing and erasing points on the screen can be increased by using the poke function to place characters in the memory positions that the screen occupies. Since the poke function moves numbers in memory rather than on the screen, faster motion can be achieved. When using the poke function, use the ASCII codes for the graphic characters and the numbers that correspond to the screen RAM in the memory of the computer. To erase or change a point, simply poke a blank character or a desired character. This substitution of characters makes the image appear to move.

Using Machine-Language and the USR Function

Probably the best way to accomplish motion on the personal computer is to use machine-language, or at least machine-language subroutines. The use of machine language bypasses the BASIC interpreter, and hence the programs run faster. Machine-language has the disadvantage of being cryptic.

The USE function is a way to call machine-language subroutines. Different computers use the USR function in different ways, but if you can use it

to increase the speed of a program, you have a faster way to display animated graphics.

An Example in BASIC—Program 25

Figures 7-1 and 7-2 are two examples of Lissajous patterns produced by the next program.

Let's look at the program. Lines 10-40 contain the title and credits. Line 45 dimensions an array so that we can actually print the figures on paper. Lines 46-49 set each element of the array to 32, the ASCII code for the blank space. In line 50 T is for the variable time, and R is the last position that we plotted. In this case it is set at the arbitrary screen position -3968. Line 60 clears the video screen.

```
10 REM               LISSAJOUS PATTERNS
20 REM           WRITTEN BY TIMOTHY J. O'MALLEY
30 REM             COPYRIGHT 1982, TAB BOOKS INC.
40 REM
45 DIM VA(30,60)
46 FOR J=0 TO 30
47 FOR K=0 TO 60
48 VA(J,K)=32
49 NEXT K,J
50 T=0:R=-3968
60 PRINT CHR$(12);
70 T=T+0.05
80 X=INT(28*SIN(2*T))
90 Y=INT(14*SIN(3*T))
95 VA((14+Y),(28+X))=43
100 P=X+64*Y-3041
110 POKE R,32
120 POKE P,43
130 R=P
135 IF T>6.3 THEN 150
140 GOTO 70
150 FOR J=0 TO 30
160 FOR K=0 TO 60
170 PRINT CHR$(VA(J,K));
180 NEXT K
190 PRINT
200 NEXT J
210 PRINT CHR$(12)
220 END
READY
```

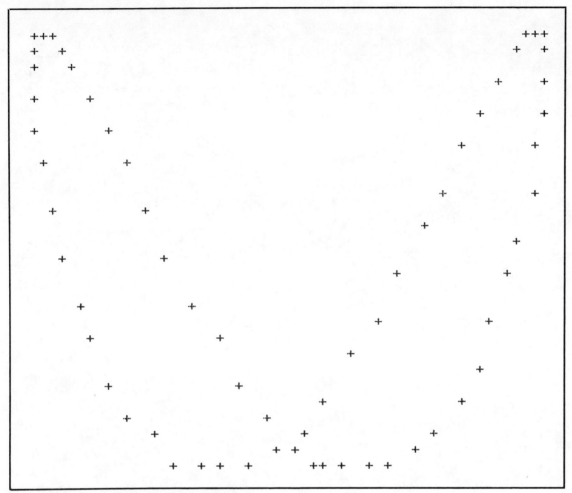

Fig. 7-1. Lissajous pattern tracing of video screen.

Line 70 increments the clock. Line 80 computes the position of the point in the horizontal direction and line 90 computes the vertical position of the point. Line 95 sets the element in the array at that position equal to 43, the ASCII code for the plus sign. Line 100 calculates the screen position using the X and Y values and assigns the value of the position to the variable P. Line 110 pokes the last position of the point R with the number 32. This erases the last plus sign. Line 120 then pokes the plus sign into its new position P. Line 130 sets the last position equal to the current position. Line 135 says that if the variable T is greater than 6.3, go to line 150, which will print out all the positions that the program

generated. If you deleted line 135, you would simply have a continuous pattern generated on the screen. Line 140 is a goto statement, which directs the computer to line 70. Lines 150-200 form nested loops that print the Lissajous pattern on paper. Line 210 causes a form feed to the next page, and line 220 ends the program.

By changing the definitions of X and Y in the program, you can generate any number of Lissajous patterns. Some computers might use the set and reset functions instead of the poke function to place dots on the video screen. This program could even be converted to create high-resolution graphics for some spectacular images. The −3968 in line 50 is

135

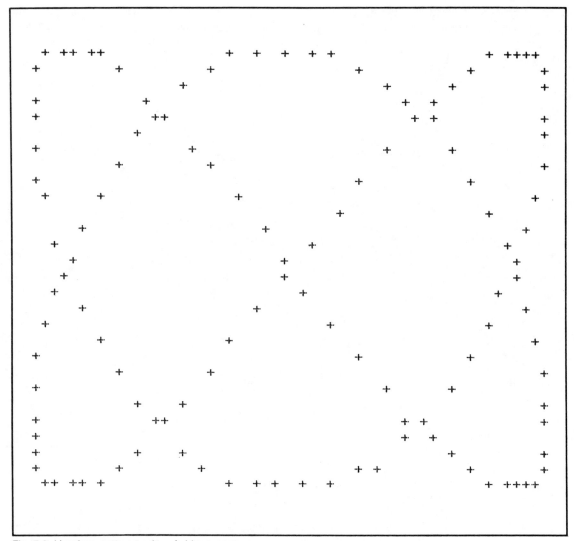

Fig. 7-2. Lissajous pattern tracing of video screen.

the screen position for the upperleft corner of the screen. Your computer might use a different number for that screen-RAM memory location. The −3041 in line 100 is the memory location for the position that is approximately in the center of the screen. Again, you may have to change that number to get a good animated graphic program.

FUTURE POSSIBILITIES

What does the future hold for graphics for personal computers? Probably a lot! Some of the things possible only on large computers will be possible on personal computers as the speed and memory of personal computers increases. There will be an amplification of some of the things that we talked about in this book and probably a lot that we didn't even hint at.

One of the things that might be possible is the creation of TV-like simulations. Your computer could generate images that change thirty times a second so that the display would look like a television picture. You could create a little world within the memory of your computer, take imaginary journeys to distant realms, and see many fascinating sights.

What else would be possible? The answer to that question lies with the imagination of the programmer and the sophistication of his computer system. Anyone who is willing to pursue a simple idea to its furthest limit will find success waiting at the end of the road. Where will it all end? I don't really know; but I do know that the sky's the limit.

Chapter 8

Advanced Graphics and Effective Video Use

In this final chapter we look at two programs in BASIC that produce graphics. In the first we see a high-resolution three-dimensional figure of a house, similar to the house program that we saw earlier. In this program the hidden perspective lines are erased. We also discuss how parts of the house can be shaded. The second program is like the molecular model that we saw earlier except we increase the efficiency of the algorithm and we apply texture, shading and highlighting to the sphere to help achieve realism in graphics. The balance of the chapter is about the effective use of the video display.

A HIGH-RESOLUTION SOLID FIGURE OF A HOUSE

The perspective line program that drew the house worked well, but it had a confusing number of lines. What we really need is a program that would not show any hidden lines. We have seen programs that use various methods to erase hidden lines. Now we look at a better algorithm for constructing a solid three-dimensional figure.

When dealing with solid figures we can no longer think in terms of lines; we must think in terms of surface polygons. A surface polygon is a flat enclosed area bounded by three or more straight lines. A cube, for instance, has six surface polygons which are all squares. The surface polygons of an object meet at their edge lines.

In our house example we must define the house as a collection of polygons. A side of a house might be one polygon; one side of a roof is another; part of the face of the house might be another. The polygons must meet the following qualifications to work in our program: (1) No interior angle of the polygon can be greater than 180 degrees; (2) no polygons can overlap each other; and (3) the physical dimensions of the polygons can not vary widely. If the interior angles exceed 180 degrees, as in a star-shaped figure, the program ignores certain parts and would probably recognize only the center of the polygon. Polygons that overlap are confusing to the algorithm although they would be drawn correctly at times. If the dimensions of the polygons vary wildly, the computer will have difficulty recognizing which polygon is closest to the viewpoint, because the program defines a midpoint for each of the polygons and measures the distances to the viewpoint from those midpoints. A priority level is established for each polygon based on the distance from the viewpoint to its midpoint.

Figure 8-1 shows images produced by this program. Imagine that you are standing in front of the house in the first figure. As you look at the next figures, imagine that you are walking around the left side of the house. You notice that a gable disap-

pears and the side of the house becomes evident. The roof on that side also comes into view. Finally the roof and sides of a porch appear in the back, and the gable roof that you saw on the right side in the first figure appears on the left side in the back.

What the program does when we take our imaginary walk is to sort the polygons by their distance to the viewpoint. It determines which ones are closer than the others and draws them in perspective accordingly. A priority order which changes with each view is established for the set of polygons.

```
10 REM     HIGH RESOLUTION SOLID FIGURE OF A HOUSE
20 REM          WRITTEN BY TIMOTHY J. O'MALLEY
30 REM          COPYRIGHT 1982, TAB BOOKS INC.
40 REM
50 GOSUB 200:REM INITIALIZE VARIABLES AND ARRAYS
60 GOSUB 900:REM SORT BY INCREASING DISTANCES TO MIDPOINTS
70 GOSUB 1100:REM TRANSLATE X,Y,Z TO H,V
80 GOSUB 1300:REM COMPLETE MATRIX DATA
90 GOSUB 1500:REM PRINT OUT HIGH RESOLUTION SOLID OBJECT
100 GOSUB 1800:REM FORM FEED FOR NEXT VIEW
110 GOSUB 1900:REM ROTATE POINTS ABOUT AN AXIS
120 GOTO 60:REM REPEAT PRINTING DIFFERENT VIEWS INDEFINITELY
200 REM          INITIALIZE VARIABLES AND MATRICES
210 IP=37:NP=27:TP=IP+NP
220 DIM X(TP),Y(TP),Z(TP),V(TP),H(TP),R(3),MTX(NP,8,5),PR(NP)
225 DIM DI(NP)
230 FOR J=1 TO IP
240 READ X(J),Y(J),Z(J)
250 NEXT J
260 DATA 0,0,0, 0,48,0, 36,48,0, 36,18,0, 20,18,0
270 DATA 20,0,0, 20,0,10, 0,0,10, 0,8,12, 20,8,12
280 DATA 0,8,20, 10,8,27, 20,8,20, 0,40,20
290 DATA 10,40,27, 20,40,20, 10,34,27, 20,28,20, 28,34,27
300 DATA 20,48,20, 28,48,27, 36,48,20, 36,28,20, 28,28,27
310 DATA 20,28,12, 36,28,12, 36,18,10, 20,18,10, 20,48,0
320 DATA 20,40,12, 20,48,10, 0,48,10, 0,40,12, 0,40,0
330 DATA 0,8,0, 20,8,0, 36,28,0
340 FOR J=1 TO NP:READ MTX(J,0,0):FOR K=1 TO MTX(J,0,0)
350 READ MTX(J,K,0):NEXT K,J
360 FOR J=1 TO NP:X1=0:Y1=0:Z1=0:FOR K=1 TO MTX(J,0,0)-1
370 X1=X1+X(MTX(J,K,0)):Y1=Y1+Y(MTX(J,K,0))
380 Z1=Z1+Z(MTX(J,K,0)):NEXT K:X(J+IP)=X1/(MTX(J,0,0)-1)
390 Y(J+IP)=Y1/(MTX(J,0,0)-1):Z(J+IP)=Z1/(MTX(J,0,0)-1)
```

```
400 NEXT J
410 DATA 5, 4,27,26,37,4
420 DATA 5, 6,7,10,36,6
430 DATA 6, 10,13,18,25,28,10
440 DATA 7, 9,11,14,33,34,35,9
450 DATA 5, 2,32,33,34,2
460 DATA 5, 2,29,31,32,2
470 DATA 6, 14,15,16,30,33,14
480 DATA 6, 3,22,23,26,37,3
490 DATA 5, 1,8,9,35,1
500 DATA 5, 16,30,31,20,16
510 DATA 5, 30,31,32,33,30
520 DATA 5, 12,13,18,17,12
530 DATA 5, 25,26,27,28,25
540 DATA 5, 5,4,27,28,5
550 DATA 4, 15,16,17,15
560 DATA 6, 3,22,21,20,29,3
570 DATA 6, 9,11,12,13,10,9
580 DATA 5, 7,8,9,10,7
590 DATA 5, 5,28,10,36,5
610 DATA 5, 1,6,7,8,1
620 DATA 5, 11,12,15,14,11
630 DATA 4, 17,18,19,17
640 DATA 4, 16,17,19,16
650 DATA 5, 24,23,22,21,24
660 DATA 4, 24,19,18,24
670 DATA 5, 19,21,20,16,19
680 DATA 6, 17,25,26,23,24,18
690 R(1)=18:R(2)=24:R(3)=14:REM  ROTATION POINT COORDINATES
700 X(0)=6:Y(0)=-100:Z(0)=6:REM  VIEWPOINT COORDINATES
710 F=0.1:G=.99:REM F IS DISTORTION AND G IS MAGNIFICATION
720 B$="Z":REM AXIS OF ROTATION
730 WID=80:W2=80:REM WID IS WIDTH OF PLOT IN PIXELS
740 E=0.4:REM ROTATION INCREMENT IN RADIANS
750 HGT=96:REM HGT IS HEIGHT OF PLOT IN PIXELS
760 GOSUB 800:REM SET UP MACHINE LANGUAGE SUBROUTINE
    FOR PRINTER
770 RETURN
800 REM      SET UP MACHINE LANGUAGE SUBROUTINE FOR PRINTER
810 POKE 260,0:POKE 261,0:REM SUBROUTINE STARTS AT 0000 HEX.
820 POKE 0,62:POKE 1,27:REM   LD A,27
830 POKE 2,205:POKE 3,12:POKE 4,224:REM   CALL SEND (AT E00C
    HEX)
840 POKE 5,201:REM     RET
850 XX=USR(0):REM  SENDS 27 TO PRINTER AT ADDRESS E00C HEX
860 POKE 1,65:XX=USR(0):REM   SENDS 65 TO PRINTER
```

```
870 POKE 1,1:XX=USR(0):REM    SENDS 1 TO PRINTER
880 RETURN
900 REM SORT BY INCREASING DISTANCES TO MIDPOINTS
910 FOR J=1 TO NP:REM DETERMINE DISTANCE TO MIDPOINTS
920 DY=Y(J+IP)-Y(0):IF DY<=0 THEN 1010:REM TOO CLOSE!!
930 DX=X(J+IP)-X(0):DZ=Z(J+IP)-Z(0)
940 DI(J)=SQR(DX*DX+DY*DY+DZ*DZ):PR(J)=J:NEXT J
950 FOR J=1 TO NP-1:K=J:REM SORT MIDPOINT DISTANCES
960 IF DI(K+1)>=DI(K) THEN 1000
970 A=PR(K):PR(K)=PR(K+1):PR(K+1)=A:REM SWITCH PRIORITY
980 A=DI(K):DI(K)=DI(K+1):DI(K+1)=A:REM SWITCH DISTANCES
990 K=K-1:IF K>0 THEN 960
1000 NEXT J:RETURN
1010 REM   TOO CLOSE!! (NOT ALL OF OBJECT CAN BE DISPLAYED)
1020 PRINT "TOO CLOSE TO OBJECT. DECREASE Y(0) IN LINE 700."
1030 PRINT "THEN TRY AGAIN."
1040 END
1100 REM          TRANSLATE X,Y,Z TO H,U
1110 FOR J=1 TO TP:DY=Y(J)-Y(0):IF DY<=0 THEN 1010:REM TOO
     CLOSE
1120 DX=X(J)-X(0):DZ=Z(J)-Z(0):U(J)=ATN(F*DZ/DY)
1130 H(J)=ATN(F*DX/DY):NEXT J:MINU=U(1):MAXU=U(1):MINH=H(1)
1140 MAXH=H(1):FOR J=1 TO TP:IF U(J)<MINU THEN MINU=U(J)
1150 IF U(J)>MAXU THEN MAXU=U(J)
1160 IF H(J)<MINH THEN MINH=H(J)
1170 IF H(J)>MAXH THEN MAXH=H(J)
1180 NEXT J
1190 DH=MAXH-MINH:DU=MAXU-MINU
1200 FOR J=1 TO TP
1210 H(J)=G*(H(J)-MINH)/DH*WID:U(J)=G*(U(J)-MINU)/DU*HGT
1220 NEXT J:RETURN
1300 REM            COMPLETE MATRIX DATA
1310 FOR J=1 TO NP:FOR K=1 TO MTX(PR(J),0,0)-1
1320 HH=H(MTX(PR(J),K+1,0))-H(MTX(PR(J),K,0))
1330 UU=U(MTX(PR(J),K+1,0))-U(MTX(PR(J),K,0))
1340 SN=SGN(HH):IF SN=0 THEN 1400:REM SLOPE EQUALS INFINITY
1350 M=UU/HH:B=U(MTX(PR(J),K,0))-M*H(MTX(PR(J),K,0))
1360 MTX(PR(J),K,1)=0:MTX(PR(J),K,2)=M
1370 MTX(PR(J),K,3)=B:MTX(PR(J),K,4)=0
1380 MTX(PR(J),K,5)=SGN((M*H(IP+PR(J))+B)-U(IP+PR(J)))
1390 NEXT K,J:RETURN
1400 REM            SLOPE EQUALS INFINITY
1410 MTX(PR(J),K,1)=1:MTX(PR(J),K,4)=H(MTX(PR(J),K,0))
1420 MTX(PR(J),K,5)=SGN(MTX(PR(J),K,4)-H(IP+PR(J)))
1430 GOTO 1390
1500 REM          PRINT OUT HIGH RESOLUTION SOLID
```

```
1510 MV=0:FOR J=1 TO TP:IF V(J)>MV THEN MV=V(J)
1520 NEXT J:MV=INT(MV)+1:REM SEARCH FOR TOP OF OBJECT
1530 FOR JS=MV TO 0 STEP -1
1540 FOR LS=0 TO INT(WID/W2)-1:GOSUB 1650:REM READY PRINTER
1550 FOR KS=LS*W2 TO LS*W2+W2-1:NS=1:MS=1:SS=0
1560 IF MTX(PR(NS),MS,1)=1 THEN 1680
1570 ZV=MTX(PR(NS),MS,2)*KS+MTX(PR(NS),MS,3)
1580 IF ZV-JS>=0 AND ZV-JS<1 THEN SS=1:GOTO 1600
1590 IF SGN(ZV-JS)<>MTX(PR(NS),MS,5) THEN 1730
1600 MS=MS+1:IF MS<MTX(PR(NS),0,0) THEN 1560
1610 POKE 1,SS:XX=USR(0)
1620 NEXT KS,LS
1630 POKE 1,13:XX=USR(0):REM NEXT LINE (CARRIAGE RETURN)
1640 NEXT JS:RETURN
1650 REM                READY PRINTER
1660 POKE 1,27:XX=USR(0):POKE 1,75:XX=USR(0):POKE 1,W2
1670 XX=USR(0):POKE 1,0:XX=USR(0):RETURN
1680 REM                VERTICAL LINE COMPARISON
1690 ZV=MTX(PR(NS),MS,4)
1700 IF ZV-KS>=0 AND ZV-KS<1 THEN SS=1:GOTO 1600
1710 IF SGN(ZV-KS)<>MTX(PR(NS),MS,5) THEN 1730
1720 GOTO 1600
1730 NS=NS+1:SS=0:MS=1:IF NS>NP THEN 1610
1740 GOTO 1560
1800 REM                FORM FEED FOR NEXT VIEW
1810 POKE 1,12:XX=USR(0):REM SEND FORM FEED CHARACTER
     TO PRINTER
1820 RETURN
1900 REM                ROTATE POINTS ABOUT AN AXIS
1910 FOR J=1 TO TP
1920 IF B$="Z" THEN A1=X(J):A2=R(1):A3=Y(J):A4=R(2)
1930 IF B$="Y" THEN A1=X(J):A2=R(1):A3=Z(J):A4=R(3)
1940 IF B$="X" THEN A1=Y(J):A2=R(2):A3=Z(J):A4=R(3)
1950 P1=A1-A2:P2=A3-A4
1960 L=SQR(P1*P1+P2*P2)
1970 IF P2=0 THEN A5=-(P1<0)*3.141593
1980 IF P1=0 THEN A5=SGN(P2)*1.570796
1990 IF P2<>0 AND P1<>0 THEN A5=ATN(P2/P1)-(P1<0)*3.141593
2000 A5=A5+E
2010 IF B$="Z" THEN X(J)=L*COS(A5)+R(1):Y(J)=L*SIN(A5)+R(2)
2020 IF B$="Y" THEN X(J)=L*COS(A5)+R(1):Z(J)=L*SIN(A5)+R(3)
2030 IF B$="X" THEN Y(J)=L*COS(A5)+R(2):Z(J)=L*SIN(A5)+R(3)
2040 NEXT J:RETURN
READY
```

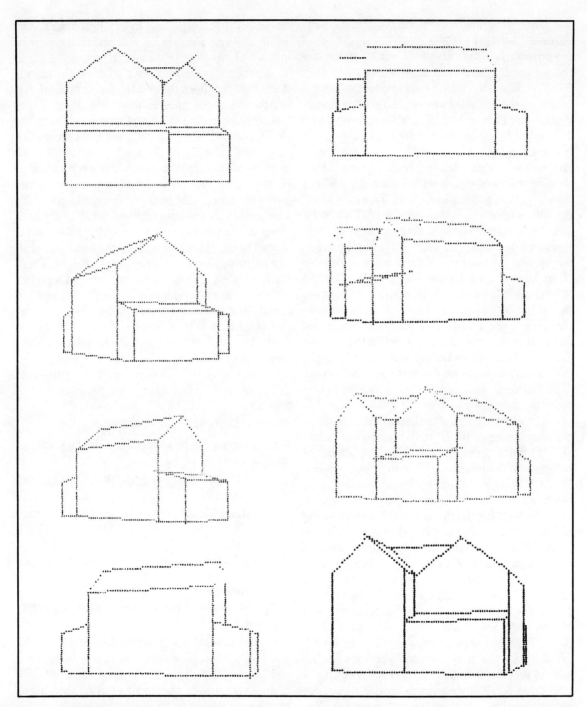

Fig. 8-1. Perspective line drawing of a house with hidden lines erased (eight views).

This program contains seven main subroutines, found in lines 200-2040. The main body of the program is in lines 10-120. Lines 10-40 identify the program. Line 50 is a subroutine call to lines 200-770, where the data is read into arrays and the values of the variables are set. Line 60 is a subroutine call to lines 900-1040 where the polygons are sorted by distances to midpoints. Line 70 is a subroutine call to line 1100 where the three-dimensional coordinates are translated to a two-dimensional perspective set of points. Line 80 is a subroutine call to lines 1300-1430. This subroutine completes or redefines the data in the MTX matrix. The MTX matrix contains data on point connections, slopes and intercepts of lines between points, and the positions of the midpoints relative to the lines of the polygons. Line 90 is a call to the subroutine in lines 1500-1740, which prints out the figure in high-resolution. Line 100 calls the subroutine in lines 1800-1820 which cause a form feed to position the next sheet of paper in the printer. Line 110 is a call to lines 1900-2040 where the points and midpoints for the next view are rotated. Line 120 sends program control to line 60 to continue the process.

Let's look at some of the important lines in this program. In line 210, IP is the number of points (X,Y,Z) in the program, and NP is the number of polygons in the program. TP is their sum. In line 220, PR is an array that holds the priority, i.e., relative closeness to viewpoint, of the polygons. Lines 260-330 contain the X, Y, and Z coordinates of the IP points. Lines 340-440 define a midpoint for each polygon by finding the mathematical average of the coordinates of the points of the polygon. Lines 410-680 define the polygons. Take, for example, line 410, which contains the data for the first polygon. Using that data the computer will draw a line from point 4 to point 27 to point 26 to point 37 and back to point 4 again. These are boundary lines for the first polygon. The data for the second polygon is in line 420 and so forth.

Lines 800-880 are a simple machine-language subroutine that sends number to the printer. You can substitute a BASIC subroutine or another subroutine if you like. This routine was used because some BASIC interpreters insert a carriage return after a given number of characters have been printed. Lines 1500-1640 search for the top of the figure (to save time) and then print out the object. Line 1560 is a check to see if the line is vertical. If it is, the computer goes to line 1680. If not ZV is calculated from the slope and intercept data in the MTX matrix. ZV is the correct vertical position (for that line for the pixel KS. Line 1580 says that if the pixel is in the current polygon line, set SS equal to 1, then goto line 1600. Line 1600 increases the polygon line counter by 1 and checks to see if the counter MS, is less than what we said the number of lines in the polygon were originally. (Remember lines 410-680?) If the pixel is on the same side of all the polygon lines as the midpoint is, then SS is sent to the printer. If SS is 1, a dot is printed; if SS is 0, a space is printed (an empty dot). Line 1590 checks to see if the pixel is one the same side as the midpoint. If a pixel ever fails to be on the same side as the midpoint, we check the next sorted polygon. If the pixel does not lie within any polygon, an empty dot is printed and we move to the next pixel position. NS is the polygon counter in the program.

Possible Changes to the Program

Polygons can be shaded by adding the following lines:

```
765   GOSUB 2100: REM READ SHADING
      DATA
2100  REM READ SHADING DATA
2110  FOR J=1 TO NP:READ CR(J):NEXT
      J:RETURN
2120  DATA (NP number of values between 0 and
      1)
227   DIM CR(NP)
1605  IF SS=0 THEN SS=(CR(PR(NS))RND
      (1))*-1
```

Here line 2120 contains numbers that tell what percentage of the pixels are to be dark, 0 being none and 1 being 100%. Line 1605 changes an empty dot to a dark dot (inside a polygon) a certain percentage of the time according to the data in line 2120.

Another possible alteration is to change the dark pixels of a line to white in order to create polygons that appear to have interior angles greater than 180 degrees. Actually you would use more than one polygon, but simply erase the lines separating them. This change could be very useful for applications in which you must use large interior angles. You can also change the program by changing the width, WID, and the height, HGT, of the plot in pixels.

A HIGH-RESOLUTION MOLECULAR MODEL

We now look at a program similar to the one we saw in Chapter 3, except this one has spheres that are textured, highlighted, and shaded. The rest of the features are the same.

Figure 8-2 shows spheres that appear to be light near the center and dark near the edges. The illusion is that light is coming from behind you as you look at the spheres. The spheres also appear to have a rough texture, although that is lessened the larger the spheres become. Again, the parts of the spheres that are hidden are not printed. As in the other program, the left side of the model appears to

```
10 REM            HIGH-RESOLUTION, SPACE-FILLING
20 REM              ROTATING MOLECULAR MODEL
30 REM            WRITTEN BY TIMOTHY J. O'MALLEY
40 REM            COPYRIGHT 1982, TAB BOOKS INC.
50 REM
60 GOSUB 100:REM INITIALIZE PROGRAM AND READ DATA
70 GOSUB 200:REM SORT BY DECREASING DISTANCES TO VIEWPOINT
80 GOSUB 400:REM PLOT POINTS AND PRINT ON PAPER
85 GOSUB 800:REM FORM FEED FOR NEXT VIEW
90 GOSUB 600:REM ROTATE POINTS ABOUT AN AXIS
95 GOTO 70:REM REPEAT ROTATION AND PRINTING INDEFINITELY
100 REM           INITIALIZE PROGRAM AND READ DATA
110 E=0.4:N1=12:RD=0.5:F=0.1:G=0.99:HGT=192:WID=160:W2=80
120 DIM X(N1),Y(N1),Z(N1),U(N1),H(N1),RS(N1),DI(N1),R(3)
130 FOR J=1 TO N1:READ X(J),Y(J),Z(J):NEXT J
140 DATA 0,0,0, 0.5,0,0.87, 1.5,0,0.87, 2,0,0
150 DATA 1.5,0,-0.87, 0.5,0,-0.87, 3,0,0, 3.5,0.348,0.348
160 DATA 4.5,0.348,0.348, 5,0,0, 4.5,-0.348,-0.348
170 DATA 3.5,-0.348,-0.348
180 GOSUB 510:REM SET UP MACHINE LANGUAGE SUBROUTINE
    FOR PRINTER
190 R(1)=2.5:R(2)=0:R(3)=0:X(0)=2.5:Y(0)=-10:Z(0)=1:B$="Z"
195 RETURN
200 REM            SORT BY DECREASING DISTANCES TO VIEWPOINT
202 FOR J=1 TO N1
204 DY=Y(J)-Y(0):IF DY<=0 THEN PRINT"DECREASE Y(0)":STOP
206 DX=X(J)-X(0):DZ=Z(J)-Z(0)
208 DI(J)=SQR(DY*DY+DX*DX+DZ*DZ):RS(J)=ATN(F*RD/DI(J))
209 U(J)=ATN(F*DZ/DY):H(J)=ATN(F*DX/DY):NEXT J
210 FOR J=1 TO N1-1:K=J
220 IF DI(K+1)<=DI(K) THEN 270
230 A=X(K):X(K)=X(K+1):X(K+1)=A:A=Y(K):Y(K)=Y(K+1):Y(K+1)=A
240 A=Z(K):Z(K)=Z(K+1):Z(K+1)=A:A=U(K):U(K)=U(K+1):U(K+1)=A
```

```
250 A=H(K):H(K)=H(K+1):H(K+1)=A:A=RS(K):RS(K)=RS(K+1):
    RS(K+1)=A
255 A=DI(K):DI(K)=DI(K+1):DI(K+1)=A
260 K=K-1:IF K>0 THEN 220
270 NEXT J
280 MINU=U(1)-RS(1):MAXU=U(1)+RS(1)
285 MINH=H(1)-RS(1):MAXH=H(1)+RS(1)
290 FOR J=1 TO N1
300 IF U(J)-RS(J)<MINU THEN MINU=U(J)-RS(J)
310 IF U(J)+RS(J)>MAXU THEN MAXU=U(J)+RS(J)
320 IF H(J)-RS(J)<MINH THEN MINH=H(J)-RS(J)
330 IF H(J)+RS(J)>MAXH THEN MAXH=H(J)+RS(J)
340 NEXT J:DH=MAXH-MINH:DU=MAXU-MINU
350 FOR J=1 TO N1
360 H(J)=G*(H(J)-MINH)/DH*WID:U(J)=G*(U(J)-MINU)/DU*HGT
370 RS(J)=G*RS(J)/DH*WID:NEXT J:RETURN
400 REM          PLOT POINTS AND PRINT ON PAPER
405 MV=0:FOR J=1 TO N1:IF U(J)+RS(J)>MV THEN MV=U(J)+RS(J)
406 NEXT J:MV=INT(MV)+1
410 FOR JS=MV TO 0 STEP -1
420 FOR LS=0 TO INT(WID/W2)-1:GOSUB 490
430 FOR KS=LS*W2 TO LS*W2+W2-1:SS=0:NS=N1
440 KH=KS-H(NS):JU=JS-U(NS):PS=SQR(KH*KH+JU*JU)
450 PZ=PS-RS(NS):IF PZ>1 THEN NS=NS-1:ON 1+SGN(NS) GOTO
    460,440
453 IF PZ<1 THEN SS=1
455 IF PZ<0 THEN SS=SGN(INT(RND(1)*RS(NS)/ABS(PZ*2)))
460 POKE 1,SS:XX=USR(0):NEXT KS,LS
470 POKE 1,13:XX=USR(0):NEXT JS
480 RETURN
490 POKE 1,27:XX=USR(0):POKE 1,75:XX=USR(0):POKE 1,W2
500 XX=USR(0):POKE 1,0:XX=USR(0):RETURN
510 REM          SET UP MACHINE LANGUAGE SUBROUTINE FOR PRINTER
520 POKE 260,0:POKE 261,0:POKE 0,62:POKE 1,27:POKE 2,205
530 POKE 3,12:POKE 4,224:POKE 5,201:XX=USR(0):POKE 1,65
540 XX=USR(0):POKE 1,1:XX=USR(0):RETURN
600 REM          ROTATE POINTS ABOUT AN AXIS
610 FOR J=1 TO N1
620 IF B$="Z" THEN A1=X(J):A2=R(1):A3=Y(J):A4=R(2)
630 IF B$="Y" THEN A1=X(J):A2=R(1):A3=Z(J):A4=R(3)
640 IF B$="X" THEN A1=Y(J):A2=R(2):A3=Z(J):A4=R(3)
650 P1=A1-A2:P2=A3-A4
660 L=SQR(P1*P1+P2*P2)
670 IF P2=0 THEN A5=-(P1<0)*3.141593
680 IF P1=0 THEN A5=SGN(P2)*1.570796
690 IF P2<>0 AND P1<>0 THEN A5=ATN(P2/P1)-(P1<0)*3.141593
```

```
700 A5=A5+E
710 IF B$="Z" THEN X(J)=L*COS(A5)+R(1):Y(J)=L*SIN(A5)+R(2)
720 IF B$="Y" THEN X(J)=L*COS(A5)+R(1):Z(J)=L*SIN(A5)+R(3)
730 IF B$="X" THEN Y(J)=L*COS(A5)+R(2):Z(J)=L*SIN(A5)+R(3)
740 NEXT J:RETURN
800 REM          FORM FEED FOR NEXT VIEW
810 POKE 1,12:XX=USR(0):RETURN
READY
```

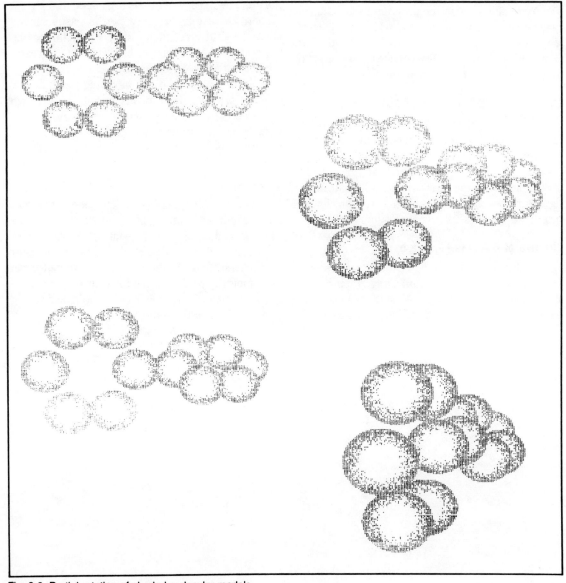

Fig. 8-2. Partial rotation of shaded molecular models.

swing toward the observer as you look at the figures.

This program is identical to Program 7 with the exception of lines 453 and 455. What these lines do is to print a dark pixel as the edge of the sphere is approached. That is, the likelihood that a pixel will be printed is greater as the pixel is closer to the circumference of the sphere; the probability is zero at the center and 100% at the edge.

You could change the program to make some spheres darker than others, to make some spheres larger than others, or to alter the height and width of the image. You could also change the direction of rotation or rotate only part of the figure.

USING THE VIDEO SCREEN EFFECTIVELY

When using the video screen on a microcomputer a crucial factor is speed. Hidden line algorithms are notorious for being slow-working "number crunchers." An effective video display should not bore the user while he is waiting for figures to appear on the screen. We will discuss briefly some ways to circumvent this problem.

The Use of Machine Language

BASIC is really not the best language to use if one wants to write a program using graphics real-time; machine-language is. Machine-language has the drawback of being very difficult to program. You can, however, solve this obstacle by using machine-language subroutines liberally througout a BASIC program. Simple but slow routines could be changed to machine-language and the rest could be left in BASIC. Every bit helps (no pun intended).

Sprites

Many newer microcomputers use *sprites*. Sprites are a group of pixels organized like a giant graphic character, but they can be easily moved about the entire screen, not simply from line to line as graphic characters can be. Their use greatly increases the speed of display.

Sprites also have the advantage of being of ordered priority. This means that if parts of two sprites occupy the same area on the screen, the one with the greater priority will be displayed on top of the other one. Sprites can have colors as well.

Other Techniques

Other techniques to increase speed of display include setting up the graphics internally while the user is reading text at the start of a program or game; using the INKEY$ function or another keyboard scanning routine so that the computer can be computing while waiting for your response; reducing computation as much as possible; and saving figures and data in memory.

Index